LET'S STUDY PHILIPPIANS

Let's Study

PHILIPPIANS

Sinclair B. Ferguson

THE BANNER OF TRUTH TRUST

THE BANNER OF TRUTH TRUST
3 Murrayfield Road, Edinburgh EH12 6EL
P.O. Box 621, Carlisle, Pennsylvania 17013, USA

*

© Sinclair B. Ferguson 1997
First Published 1997
ISBN 0 85151 714 5

*

Typeset in 11/12pt Ehrhardt MT
at the Banner of Truth Trust, Edinburgh
Printed and bound in Finland by
WSOY – Book Printing Division

*

Scripture quotations are from the *Holy Bible: New International Version*
(NIV), copyright ©1973, 1978, 1984, by International Bible Society.
Used by permission of Zondervan Publishing House.

Contents

Preface

Let's Study Philippians is part of a projected series of books which explain and apply the message of Scripture. The series is designed to meet a specific and important need in the church. While not technical commentaries, each volume will comment on the text of a biblical book; and while not merely lists of practical applications, they are concerned with the ways in which the teaching of Scripture can affect and transform our lives today. Understanding the Bible's message and applying its teaching are the aims.

Like other volumes in the series, *Let's Study Philippians* seeks to combine explanation and application. Its concern is to be helpful to ordinary Christian people by encouraging them to understand the message of the Bible and apply it to their own lives. The reader in view is not the person who is interested in all the detailed questions which fascinate the scholar, although behind the writing of each study lies an appreciation for careful and detailed scholarship. The aim is exposition of Scripture written in the language of a friend, seated alongside you with an open Bible.

Let's Study Philippians is designed to be used in various contexts. It can be used simply as an aid for individual Bible study. Some may find it helpful to use in their devotions with husband or wife, or to read in the context of the whole family.

In order to make these studies more useful, not only for individual use but also for group study in Sunday School classes and home, church or college, study guide material will be found on pp. 119–135. Sometimes we come away frustrated rather than helped by group discussions. Frequently that is because we have been encouraged to discuss a passage of Scripture which we do not understand very well in the first place. Understanding must always be the foundation for enriching discussion and thoughtful, practical application. Thus, in addition to the exposition of Philippians, the additional material provides questions to encourage personal thought and study, or to be used as discussion starters. The Group Study Guide divides the material into thirteen sections and provides direction for leading and participating in group study and discussion.

The text which forms the basis of the studies is *The New International Version.*

Philippians is a wonderful book to study. In reading and studying it again in a concentrated period I have once more come to appreciate its riches and been thankful for its teaching. My prayer is that this experience will be shared by others who read these pages.

SINCLAIR B. FERGUSON
Westminster Theological Seminary
Philadelphia, Pennsylvania

The Philippian Church

One afternoon around twenty years after the crucifixion of Jesus of Nazareth, a small group of travellers made their way in a north-westerly direction from the port of Neapolis, where they had recently landed from Troas. They journeyed, presumably on foot, for a further ten miles or so along the great Roman road called the Via Egnatia until they came to the city of Philippi.

Many people probably passed that little group of travellers without giving any of them a second look, not realising that these were men who were gaining the reputation of having 'caused trouble all over the world' (*Acts* 17:6). They included Silas, the young Timothy, and, apparently, Luke the medical doctor. (He seems to have joined them at Troas, as the change from the use of 'they' in Acts 16:8 to 'we' in Acts 16:10ff suggests.) Their leader was, of course, the apostle Paul.

THE GOSPEL COMES TO EUROPE

In this modest fashion, Paul's mission team, with its message of Jesus Christ as crucified and risen Saviour and Lord, moved for the first time to 'European' soil.

Unprepossessing their arrival may have been, but they were as certain that God had called them there as they were of their own existence. He had given them clear direction.

They had needed special guidance from God because preaching the gospel in Philippi was no part of their original plan. They had travelled throughout Phrygia and Galatia and seem to have planned to go into the province of Asia. But in some supernatural manner (perhaps through a prophetic utterance, or some obvious divine providence) they were kept from doing so. Later they tried to cross the border between Mysia and Bithynia, but were again prevented by some Spirit-inspired intimation. They therefore moved on and soon found themselves in Troas (*Acts* 16:6–8).

This was an unusual experience for this small group of travelling missionaries. They were, no doubt, perplexed about the significance of these restrictions which God seemed to have placed on their movements. But the perplexity did not last long. During that first night in Troas, Paul had a vision. In it he saw a man from Macedonia, on the other side of the Aegean Sea. He stood there, begging, 'Come over to Macedonia and help us.'

Luke's record of what followed is both interesting and instructive. The missionary band paused momentarily to assess the significance of Paul's experience. In his narrative at Acts 16:10, Luke uses a verb (translated 'concluded' in the NIV) which has the root idea of placing one thing down alongside another. They placed side-by-side (i) the ways in which God seemed to have closed doors and (ii) this unusual night vision. How should they interpret these events? There was unanimous agreement: 'God is surely calling us to Macedonia to preach the gospel there too.'

They obeyed this heavenly vision; a wind-assisted crossing brought them quickly to the island of Samothrace and then on to the port of Neapolis. From there they headed for the major city in the area: Philippi.

IN THE CITY OF PHILIPPI

Philippi was founded in the middle of the fourth century before Christ and named after Philip II of Macedonia, the father of the famous Alexander the Great. It was later conquered by the Romans in the mid-second century before Christ, and in 42 B.C. it had become, as Luke tells us, 'a Roman colony' (*Acts* 16:12). It was, in many respects, a kind of 'miniature Rome'. It was ruled by Roman law, and reflected Roman life-style, politically, socially and even architecturally.

Here, then, Paul came with his companions – all men with one aim: to preach the gospel of Christ to all who would listen, whatever the consequences.

Their first visit was relatively brief, but action-packed. By the first Sabbath after they had settled in the city, they had discovered that there was no synagogue in Philippi.

Paul's practice in spreading the gospel in a new city was always to go first to the synagogue (*Rom.* 1:16–17). When invited as a visitor to address the congregation, he would take the opportunity to show from Scripture that the crucified and risen Christ was the long-awaited Messiah (see *Acts* 9:22; 13:5, 14; 14:1). The fact that no synagogue existed must have been discouraging. It meant that there were less than ten male Jews in this significant city (the number necessary to form the quorum of a synagogue).

There was no obvious bridgehead here for the gospel. But the apostolic band did uncover one sign of hope. In such circumstances, if there were any Jews or Jewish proselytes in the city, they might meet together for prayer at the riverside, perhaps remembering the days of the exile in Babylon (see *Psa.* 137; *Ezek.* 1:1–3).

Here, beside the river, they found a small group of women (*Acts* 16:13). These were the people the Lord had prepared. When Paul spoke, one particular heart was opened; others joined her.

The first convert, Lydia by name, was a business woman with servants and a substantial home. She graciously invited the apostolic missionaries to share her home and to receive her hospitality. While the first Christians continued to meet at the riverside, it was probably in this house, the home of Lydia, that the first church in Philippi began to meet (*Acts* 16:14–15). Two other women who were perhaps converted at that time were named Euodia and Syntyche. They would later exercise very significant ministries in the church. Apart from Epaphroditus, who brought Paul's letter to the Philippians, the only man whose name we know was Clement.

This must have seemed one of the quietest beginnings to the life of a church Paul had ever experienced. But it was simply the calm before the storm.

Shortly afterwards Paul found it necessary to risk the security of the missionary band, and even the future of their work in Philippi. He destroyed the trade of an unscrupulous group of men who mercilessly used a demon-possessed girl for financial gain as a fortune-teller. She had followed the apostolic band through the streets, shouting at them: 'These men are servants of the Most High God, who are telling you the way to be saved' (*Acts* 16:17).

The situation must have placed enormous strain on Paul. For a while he tolerated it, perhaps realising that to do anything might jeopardise the entire mission. But when this continued 'for many days' he knew it had to be stopped. He exorcised the demon in the name of Christ (*Acts* 16:18). The girl was delivered and both her taunting and her fortune-telling ceased.

Luke tantalisingly tells us no more about this girl! But of the three cameo portraits he gives of the apostolic band in Philippi two of them describe remarkable but very different conversions. He may intend us to understand that this was a third one. Here were three new members of the church, their diverse backgrounds and conversion experiences indicating just how varied that little congregation was.

In the event Paul's fears were fully realised. The owners of the girl were incensed because of their loss of income. They dragged Paul and Silas before the authorities who had them stripped and beaten and thrown into prison (*Acts* 16:22).

It was here, in the Philippian jail, that one of the most famous conversions in the history of the church took place. At midnight Paul and Silas were praying and singing praises (Paul spoke to the Philippians with the authority of experience when he encouraged them to 'Rejoice in the Lord always', *Phil.* 4:4). Suddenly the ground shook underneath them; the building began to totter; the prisoners' chains were immediately loosened from the walls. The prison doors banged open. This was an earthquake!

Life suddenly caved in on the poor jailer. His prisoners would escape; he would be held responsible. He took out his sword and was about to take his own life. But Paul shouted to him to stop, and assured him that all the prisoners were still there. Lights were called for, and the jailer rushed into the presence of Paul and Silas with the immortal question on his lips, 'What must I do to be saved?'

Had he heard the demon-possessed girl's high-pitched shouts? Or was it something he had heard these strange prisoners sing? Or did he not fully understand the significance of his own question? No matter to Paul and Silas; they seized the opportunity. 'Trust in

Christ, as we have done', they said, 'and you will be saved. Yes, and your household too.' So he was. Along with his family he was baptized. There was joy in Philippi that night (*Acts* 16:34)!

Morning came, and with it a self-assured message from the magistrates that one night's confinement was enough for these travelling preachers; they were free; but free only to leave town. This the magistrates had the power to enforce. But before they did, Paul had something to say. He, a Roman citizen, had been beaten publicly and imprisoned without due process of law. Let the magistrates themselves come to escort the apostolic band out of town!

No doubt Paul guessed the alarm this news would create; a grave miscarriage of justice had taken place. The shrewd apostle knew they would come immediately and do as he said.

It would be some time before the citizens of Philippi would forget the day the city fathers had eaten humble-pie and given a civic escort to travelling evangelists whom they had had beaten the day before! It must have provided something of a talking point. Paul was leaving behind many opportunities to explain who these men really were and why they had come to the city of Philippi.

A LASTING RELATIONSHIP

Paul did not forget the Philippians; neither did they forget him. They supported his ministry (*2 Cor.* 11:7–10; *Phil.* 4:15–16). Later Paul returned to Macedonia, encouraging the young churches and continuing his travels into Greece; the return journey, contrary to his original plan, took him back the way he had come, once more through Philippi (*Acts* 20:1–6). His love for the Philippians continued as their appreciation of him grew in return. A special bond was formed, not only between Paul and the Philippians, but probably also between the Philippians and Timothy as well.

During this journey in which Paul had revisited the Philippians (often called his third missionary journey) he had been spreading a burden among the Gentile churches which he hoped would seal their unity in Christ with their Jewish fellow-believers. He organised a collection to help the impoverished church in Jerusalem.

This goal was fulfilled (*Acts* 24:17). But while in Jerusalem Paul was arrested. In the process of his court hearings he was transferred to confinement in Caesarea; two years or so later he exercised his right to appeal to Caesar and around the year A.D. 60 was sent to Rome where, under house arrest, he now waited his verdict.

Some time had passed since the Philippians had been able to help Paul. But now, alarmed by the seriousness of his situation, they sent a generous gift to him by the hand of one of their members, Epaphroditus. In the process of fulfilling his mandate Epaphroditus became seriously ill and almost died. Now that he was well enough to travel, Paul was sending him back with a message.

The Philippians may have had a further reason for their contact with Paul. They possibly hoped that the presence of Epaphroditus would enable Paul to release Timothy to come to help them with a number of problems which had developed in their fellowship. They had shared these with the apostle, and perhaps had even requested Timothy's help realising their situation required the kind of ministry they knew he would be able to exercise.

At a somewhat uncertain and obviously crucial stage in his life Paul could not be without Timothy. In the meantime Epaphroditus would return alone, bearing whatever pastoral counsel and encouragement Paul could give in the brief compass of a personal letter.

That letter is the one we know as 'Philippians'.

Almost two thousand years after they were written these pages continue to speak with a freshness and power. Our situation and circumstances differ from those of these early Christians; but in the message they received we hear the voice of the Spirit of God addressing us still today. It was written by Paul for 'all the saints in Philippi' (*Phil.* 1:1). It is meant by the Spirit for 'all the saints' in every age and place who 'confess that Jesus Christ is Lord, to the glory of God the Father' (*Phil.* 2:11).

Outline of Philippians

1. INTRODUCTION
   - (i) Opening Greetings (1:1–2)
   - (ii) Paul's Thanksgiving and Prayer (1:3–11)

2. THE SERVICE OF CHRIST
   - (i) To Advance the Gospel (1:12–18a)
   - (ii) Life in Christ, Life of Joy (1:18b–26)

3. A CALL TO PRACTICAL HOLINESS
   - (i) Conduct Befitting the Gospel (1:27–2:4)
   - (ii) The Mind of Christ (2:5–11)
   - (iii) Working Out Salvation (2:12–18)
   - (iv) Two Christ-Like Men (2:19–30)

4. FALSE TEACHING OR TRUE LIVING?
   - (i) A Word of Warning (3:1–4a)
   - (ii) Paul's Testimony (3:4b–11)
   - (iii) Pressing On and Up (3:12–4:1)

5. COUNSEL FOR JOYFUL LIVING
   - (i) Unity, Joy, Peace and Purity (4:2–9)
   - (ii) Gift and Gratitude (4:10–20)

6. CONCLUSION
   - Final Greetings (4:21–23)

I

Dear Philippians

Paul and Timothy, servants of Christ Jesus, To all the saints in Christ Jesus at Philippi, together with the overseers and deacons: Grace and peace to you from God our Father and the Lord Jesus Christ (Phil. 1:1–2).

Many Christians find Philippians the most attractive of all Paul's letters – and the easiest part of his writings to read. In a way that is not surprising. But at first glance the opening words read like any other letter Paul wrote. It is tempting to glance at them and quickly read on.

Yet it is worth pausing to read Paul's words again, for everything he says is weighted with significance.

GREETINGS

Letters in the ancient world, as in the modern world, tended to open in a very conventional way. But in one respect at least, the style was more sensible than ours. When we write letters we do not give our name until the very last word. Sometimes that can prove to be frustrating (especially if we are the kind of person who uses so much of the page that the signature is written side-on in the margin!). In the ancient world, however, they followed a more sensible practice. Letters began with three words: (i) the name of the writer; (ii) the name of the recipient; (iii) 'greetings'.

Paul follows that custom, but he gives it a distinctively Christian flavour. He does not simply bring 'greetings'. He wishes *grace and peace* (v. 2).

Grace is God's love for the unworthy, revealed in the coming of Jesus and his self-giving on the cross (cf. *2 Cor.* 8:9); *peace* echoes the familiar Hebrew greeting *shalom*, spiritual and physical well-being. That is why Paul says that it comes *from God our Father and the Lord Jesus Christ.*

Two persons of the Trinity (Father and Son), are mentioned here; the third, the Holy Spirit, is implied. For it is he who brings to us the blessings which the Father and the Son store up for us (*John.* 16:15). Salvation means experiencing God's grace and peace; such blessing has its origin in the love, plan and power of the great triune God. Thus, in one simple greeting Paul assumes some of the deepest and richest truths of the Christian gospel. No ordinary greeting this!

READERS

But then the recipients of this letter are no ordinary people. Four things characterise them:

(i) They are *saints,* or 'holy ones'. This, of course, is the New Testament's word to describe every Christian (*Rom.* 1:7; *1 Cor.* 1:2; *2 Cor.* 1:2; *Eph.* 1:1). It does not refer to only certain outstanding Christians whom the church recognises in a special way by 'canonising' them. No, all Christians have had their old life 'cut off' (the root meaning of Paul's word) and are now distanced, or set apart, from their former lifestyle. They belong to Christ. In fact it is only through belonging to Christ that they have become saints.

(ii) They are *in Christ Jesus.* This (or the similar expression 'in the Lord') is Paul's favourite way of describing a Christian. He uses these expressions well over one hundred times in his letters. What does he mean by them?

It helps us to understand this phrase when we remember that Paul taught that those who are now in Christ were once 'in Adam'. The first man, Adam, was certainly an individual, but he was also appointed by God as a representative for the whole human race.

Whatever Adam did had repercussions for others. What he did counted not only for himself, but also for them. When we come to have actual life and existence, we come personally to share in the consequences of being 'in Adam' (see *Rom.* 5:12–21 for an extended explanation).

Jesus is, for Paul, the 'second man' and 'the last Adam' (*1 Cor.* 15:22, 45, 47). He came to do all that Adam failed to do, and to undo all that Adam did through his fall. In his death and resurrection he dealt with the guilt and power of sin, and with the reign of Satan (*Rom.* 4:25; *Col.* 2:13–16). When we come to trust in Christ (the New Testament's phrase is actually 'to believe *into*' Christ) we begin to share in the blessing of all that he did for us. In Christ, says Paul in his great letter to the Ephesians, God has blessed us 'with every spiritual blessing' (*Eph.* 1:3).

(iii) They are *at Philippi* (v. 1). From one point of view there is nothing unusual about that; the words seem commonplace. But notice what is implied: the Christian lives in two different orders of reality at the same time. We belong to Christ. As Paul will later say, 'our citizenship is in heaven' (3:20), not here on the earth. Yet for the moment we live in a sinful environment, 'at Philippi', or London or Atlanta. Here we are called to live as alien residents. Our emphases (accents!) and lifestyle make others say, 'Now, where do you belong?' That is effective Christian living and witness.

(iv) They are *with the overseers and deacons* (v. 1). Paul addressed them as a fellowship, a congregation of Jesus Christ, and not merely as isolated individuals.

Overseer is the literal translation of the Greek word *episkopos*, sometimes translated as 'bishop'. In the New Testament it refers to the same person as 'elder' (compare *Acts* 20:17 with 28). Elder refers to the seniority of the leader (perhaps in age, but certainly in spiritual wisdom); bishop describes the ministry he exercises: he oversees or leads his fellow-Christians.

The task of *deacons* in the New Testament church is much less clearly stated. The word means someone who serves at table. The differences in qualifications required (compare *1 Tim.* 3:8–13 with 1–7) suggest that, like the seven men who assisted the apostles in the early days of the church in Jerusalem, deacons were responsible to see that the practical affairs of church life were spiritually organised (cf. *Acts* 6:1–7).

It is interesting to notice that this is the only congregation in the New Testament Paul addresses in this way. Why did he do so? Perhaps it was to pave the way for the exhortations he would later give to unity, humility and maturity.

CORRESPONDENTS

Philippians comes from *Paul and Timothy*. Timothy is included not only because he was with Paul, but also because he was involved in the founding of the church at Philippi (*Acts* 16:1ff). He may well have had a special place in the affections of these Christians. Certainly Paul assumes they would be disappointed that he was not planning to send Timothy to them immediately (2:23).

Both men are described as *servants* [or slaves] *of Christ Jesus* (v. 1). All Christians are servants, bond-slaves of Jesus. Yet Paul uses that description of individual Christians relatively infrequently. While it is true in general that we are all Christ's servants, perhaps it is not always obvious that we are. A Christian with a tendency to 'selfish ambition', for example (2:3), hardly displays the qualities of a true servant.

But from all we know of Timothy, he was a true bond-slave of Jesus. He had served with Paul in the gospel of Christ, and Paul could point to him and call him 'servant of Jesus'.

An amazing amount of biblical teaching lies behind this simple introduction which Paul writes. It is just the kind of teaching that should encourage us to give ourselves again to Christ as his servants.

2

A Sharing Church

I thank my God every time I remember you. In all my prayers for all of you, I always pray with joy because of your partnership in the gospel from the first day until now (Phil. 1:3–5).

The relationship between a pastor and a congregation is inevitably one of the most important features in the life of a church. That is certainly true of the *founding* pastor. Sometimes, sadly, the relationship turns sour. Perhaps the congregation discovers that their leader has faults they had not noticed before when they had immaturely adored him; at other times the fault lies with certain members of the congregation who cannot tolerate the leadership of others over a long period.

Paul's relationships with the congregations he had founded were varied. Think of the problems at Corinth, and the struggles he had to keep the Galatians committed to the grace of God in the gospel!

CROWN AND JOY

Thankfully there was one congregation with which Paul enjoyed an especially harmonious relationship: Philippi! It is hardly surprising that he uses the language of joy and rejoicing so often in his letter to them (1:3, 18, 26; 2:2, 17, 29; 3:1; 4:1, 4, 10). They were his 'joy and crown' (4:1), or, as we might say, his crowning joy! If Paul had been asked to name the congregation, would he

[5]

have called it the First Joy and Crown Church of Philippi? No wonder he gave thanks to God every time he prayed for them (v. 3)!

PRAYERFUL

Notice the comprehensiveness of Paul's words: *In* all *of my prayers for* all *of you I* always *pray with joy* (v. 4)! Since he was so thankful for them we might mistakenly conclude that praying for all of them like this was a simple matter. But as the rest of the letter shows there were also aspects of the life of the church in Philippi, and even members of it, which would have caused Paul pain whenever he thought about them. But his praying is not selective (only for those who are doing well, or whom he happens to like and finds easy to get on with); nor did he allow his prayers for difficult circumstances or people to focus only on the dark side. Later he will 'plead with Euodia and . . . with Syntyche to agree with each other' (4:2); but for the moment he prays for both of them *with joy*. Perhaps that explains why he was later able to speak about them so openly and lovingly.

JOYFUL

Paul's prayers were not only thankful; they were also joyful. On other occasions his intercession was marked by agony, compassion or sorrow. But when he began to pray for this group of Christians he found his spirits were lifted; prayer came from his heart like water rushing downhill, whereas in his intercession for others he sometimes felt like a man swimming against the tide. Praying for the Philippians energised him, whereas praying for others sometimes exhausted him.

Even in an incidental comment like this, Paul teaches us about the mystery of prayer. It is not simply a listing of the requests we have; it involves entering into others' situations, needs, triumphs and failures, and carrying them into the presence of God. Praying can sometimes take a heavy toll on our emotions and leave us emptied of our strength; at other times it revives us and lifts our spirits. In either case, the great task of intercession involves our whole being.

PARTNERSHIP

But why did the Philippian church have this marked effect on Paul? Because of their *partnership in the gospel from the first day until now* (v. 5).

Partnership translates the word *koinōnia,* which means communion, participation or fellowship. We should notice three things about this:

(i)   Their partnership was gospel-centred. They shared with Paul in the great task of 'contending . . . for the faith of the gospel' (1:27); they shared too in suffering for their faith, and in seeing that suffering as a privilege (1:29); they wanted to share in Paul's 'troubles', in prayer as well as in other ways (1:19).

It is an important aspect of the New Testament's understanding of the gospel that Christ not only draws us to himself by his Spirit's work; he also draws us nearer to each other. Our commitment to Christ always implies a commitment to Christ's people (cf. *Heb.* 11:25–26). To love and care for his brothers is to love and care for him (*Matt.* 25:34–40).

(ii)   Their partnership was material and personal. Paul uses the term 'fellowship' several times in his letters when talking about the collection which the Christians in Macedonia had made for those in Jerusalem. Sometimes fellowship takes the concrete form of making a financial contribution (*Rom.* 15:26, where the word *koinōnia* is used).

We often think of fellowship as spiritual in distinction from material; we mean little more than enjoying conversation and discussion with our fellow-Christians. Paul was thankful that the Philippians' fellowship with him involved more than that. They had dug down into their personal resources and sent him a monetary gift (4:14) to help him personally and to encourage him in his ministry. They did more: they sent a person with the gift. Epaphroditus was to give Paul his personal care and attention while he was in prison (2:25). How much he must have appreciated seeing a familiar and much loved face and hearing direct news of the Philippians, as well as receiving their material support! Your

[7]

cheque book is important, but it is not all-important! It is, for example, never money wasted when we send people to encourage missionaries as well as provide them with financial support.

(iii) Their partnership was also ongoing. *From the first day until now* (v. 5) they had been committed to Paul and his ministry. Other churches seem to have waxed and waned in their affection for the apostle (and perhaps in remembering his ministry in the church budget! 4:15). But these young Christians had remained faithful to him throughout the years and had supported him whenever they had the opportunity and the resources to do so (4:10).

Being a Christian means entering into a partnership with others, to share in the work of Christ. There is, ordinarily, no such thing as an isolated Christian. We belong to those who belong to Christ! Indeed, where there is no giving, no caring, no loving, no sharing, there is no true fellowship.

In whose ministry do you have fellowship?

3

God at Work

*Being confident of this, that he who began a good work in you
will carry it on to completion until the day of Christ Jesus. It
is right for me to feel this way about all of you, since I have
you in my heart; for whether I am in chains or defending and
confirming the gospel, all of you share in God's grace with
me. God can testify how I long for all of you with the
affection of Christ Jesus* (Phil. 1:6–8).

Thinking about the Philippians filled Paul with joy. After all, he
had planted the church in Philippi as the result of a series
of remarkable circumstances. First there was the vision of the
man from Macedonia summoning him to bring the gospel to
Europe; then there was the triumph of grace that emerged from a
situation which was humanly-speaking deeply discouraging. Then
a jailer had been converted! Did that thought inevitably cheer
Paul's spirits now that he was again in prison?

But joy does not go unthreatened in the human heart. It is
assailed by niggling doubts and fears. All very well to rejoice in
what God had done in the past in these Philippians; but what
would happen to them under pressure? Would they stand firm?
Was Paul's joy in them well-grounded?

CONFIDENCE IN GOD

Paul assures the Philippians that he has every reason to be
joyful. It is not as though their Christian faith depends ultimately
on him or his ministry to them. It has a firmer, more reliable

foundation than that. The good work of the lifelong transformation of these believers has its origin in God. *He began a good work in them* (v. 6), and, Paul argues, what God begins God completes.

Later he will explain more fully *how* God does this (2:12–13). For the moment he is more interested in stressing that it is *God* who does it.

The Philippians were surely in no doubt that the work had begun with God and not with themselves. Think of Lydia's conversion: the Lord had 'opened' her heart (*Acts* 16:14). Think of the jailer; he had done nothing to inaugurate the work of salvation in his life (*Acts* 16:29–34). His conversion was as unexpected as the earthquake which led to it. Rather than being ready for the gospel, it took a heaven-ordained catastrophe to bring him to his knees.

Furthermore, these were inauspicious beginnings for a church – a women's riverside prayer meeting and the local jail! Hardly the venues we would naturally choose. But when God is at work, no circumstances are inauspicious or insignificant.

But how is Paul so confident that when God brings new life he also keeps working in us *until the day of Christ Jesus?* That last phrase gives us the clue: the reason God has begun to work in us is because he has a long-term plan. He is getting us ready to see and share in the glory of his Son.

The verb Paul uses, *carry it on to completion* suggests the idea of putting the finishing touches to. That is what God is doing in our lives. From one point of view we may seem to have a long, long way to go in growing in grace and holiness. But from another point of view the major part of the work has been done. The Philippians were already Christ's; now God was completing his great work.

It is important to notice the horizon towards which Paul is looking. We often have our gaze fixed on the end of our life, whenever that may be. Then we will be with Christ (v. 23). But Paul looks for the return of his Saviour in majesty and glory. Then the final transformation will take place in which his people will be made fully like him with transformed and resurrected bodies. Then the work of restoration and salvation which God has begun will be complete.

FEELINGS ABOUT THE PHILIPPIANS

Sometimes Christians may give the impression that they have no emotions. That was obviously not true of Paul. Here he openly confessed his feelings about his friends in Philippi. That fact itself is extraordinary when we recall the twisted spirit which character-ised his life before his conversion. Now he was like a flower opened to the sun, refreshed by the dew of heaven. He had them in his heart. He loved them, and lingered in prayer for them.

What was the explanation? In whatever activity he was engaged, in whatever situation he found himself – in prison, or preaching in the market place or in the synagogue – Paul and the Philippians were bound together by a common bond: grace. Jesus Christ had bound them to himself in love, love so amazing and divine that the only adequate response was for Paul to give his all to him. Having done that, he wanted to love anyone else who had experienced the same grace and responded in the same way.

That is true. But Paul almost certainly means more than this. He says, literally, that the Philippians are 'fellow partakers of the grace of me'. That could mean the grace which he experiences; but it may also mean the grace-gift which he possesses. They have been (literally) fellow-partakers, fellow-fellowshippers in his grace, whether he has been a prisoner, or an apologist, or an evangelist. They have been committed to supporting his ministry whatever his circumstances.

No wonder he was grateful for them! No wonder he was sure that this was a supernatural work that had begun in them! No wonder he was so full of joy when he thought about them!

What a model these Philippians are. Of course they had the privilege of sharing in the ministry of the great apostle Paul. But Paul himself makes it clear that his own life was not plain sailing. He was not always appreciated by his fellow-believers. Yet the Philippians stuck with him, whatever other churches said or did! It must have been tempting at times to forget about him; no doubt there were travelling preachers who passed through the city and tried to wean them away from him (cf. 3:2). Perhaps there were times when other leaders seemed more attractive, other preachers more eloquent than Paul (cf. *2 Cor.* 10:10). But they were committed to him; they had a pastoral bond to him.

How fickle we modern Christians are by comparison: often uncommitted, and consequently unreliable in times of difficulty, failure, or crisis in the fellowship to which we belong. When difficulties arise (of whatever kind), we seek more comfortable pastures. Not so the Philippians. No wonder such a bond of love developed between Paul and these Christians.

The bonds of grace are strengthened by adversity; the affection of the heart is deepened by sharing in suffering. This is Paul's testimony in verse eight: *God can testify how I long for all of you with the affection of Christ Jesus.* His feelings for them are so strong that he can call God as a witness to their reality. The word 'affection' refers to the intestines. His 'gut-feelings' as we might colloquially put it. This is real Christian affection.

When Christians experience the grace of God doing this to them, then people begin to say, 'See how these Christians love one another!'

4

Praying for Growth

And this is my prayer: that your love may abound more and more in knowledge and depth of insight, so that you may be able to discern what is best and may be pure and blameless until the day of Christ, filled with the fruit of righteousness that comes through Jesus Christ – to the glory and praise of God (Phil. 1:9–11).

T he introductions to Paul's letters often give us indications of the themes he will later develop and of the concerns he has for each particular fellowship to which he writes. That is certainly true of the Letter to the Philippians. Already in the opening verses he has given generous expression to his appreciation for these Christians and has shared with them the deep assurance he has that God will complete the work he had begun among them.

Human logic might reason at this point: If God has begun and will complete his work in us then we are relieved of any responsibility. It would be easy to be lulled into spiritual indifference by such reasoning. With such an assurance in his heart, Paul could surely relax his prayers for them.

But biblical and spiritual logic is more reliable than such reasoning. Our tendency is to say: If God does the work, we have nothing to do. Paul's logic is the reverse: Because God is at work, we have a responsibility to respond to his work.

This will become even clearer when the apostle returns to the same theme in 2:12–13. But here, in the early part of his letter, where he is assuring the Philippians of his prayers for them, he wants to share with them what it is that he prays. He prays for their spiritual growth. Later he will tell them how he does not rest content with his own spiritual progress (3:12–14). Here he indicates that he longs for their advance in grace as well.

GROWTH IN LOVE

Central to his concern is that his friends should grow in love. That was specially relevant to a congregation where niggling divisions were beginning to creep in (cf. 2:1ff; 4:1ff). Growth in love was essential if they were to respond in a Christ-like way to new and potentially difficult situations (and people!). In fact this is the context in which love is most likely to grow, because its presence is so urgently required. Such situations test the reality of our love and stretch it to its full potential.

To exercise the kind of love in which we put others before ourselves is so demanding that we instinctively want to know what the limits of our responsibility are. That was what lay behind the famous question Jesus was asked when he said that the great commandment was to love God and our neighbour. The query, 'Who is my neighbour?' is really a request for information that will limit our responsibilities (if he is a neighbour, I need to love him; if not, I can leave him). Jesus' reply was devastating: '*You are to be the neighbour*'; wherever there is need you have a responsibility to care; there is no limit (see *Luke* 10:25–37). There is no end to love. It can never say 'I have done enough.' That is why Paul prayed that the love of the Philippians might *abound more and more*.

But Paul does not specify the object of this love. Is it God? Is it our fellow-Christians? Is it non-Christians? But if he does not limit love's object, should we? It is 'all of the above'!

KNOWLEDGE AND DISCERNMENT

We often say that love is blind. From one point of view that is true. Love transcends human differences and divisions. But from another point of view Christian love requires vision. We need to be able to recognise need and to see what can be done in response to it. That is why love cannot grow strong unless it is in the context of increased spiritual *knowledge and depth of insight* (v. 9).

Love and insight need to go together. To love is to have the motivation to help; depth of insight enables us to see what the real need is. Love means we have compassion; insight means that we see the situation clearly and realistically. Then we are able to *discern what is best* (v. 10).

But where does such insight come from? The context gives us the answer. Paul is *praying* for this, for such insight and discernment comes only from God. It comes by divine revelation. For us today that means it comes through studying and knowing the Scriptures with the help of the Holy Spirit. As we allow the way we think and feel to be influenced by God's word, our own responses to emerging situations will become increasingly moulded by the mind and will of God. As we live in his presence, we will become more like him; we will instinctively begin to think in a biblical, that is a godly, way about people and circumstances. We will begin to 'feel' about them in a way that expresses the attitude of God's own heart.

HOLINESS

Discernment not only means that we see the needs of others; it also means we see more clearly what we ourselves need if we are to grow in Christian experience. To *discern what is best* (v. 10) probably includes the idea of choosing the best as well as recognising it. Holiness is not only a matter of the mind and our understanding; it involves the will and our commitment.

Do we really want what is best for us? The question may seem a ridiculous one. Of course we do! But do we, really? Most Christians with a little self-knowledge realise how easily they settle for second best, or even worse, in their lives. We are content with spiritual knowledge if it does not make too many demands on the level of our obedience. No wonder Paul felt the need to pray his fellow-Christians on and on to the fruit of love and knowledge: purity, blamelessness and righteousness. His concern is that their lives should be fit for the scrutiny of Jesus Christ when he returns as Lord and Judge (*until the day of Christ,* v. 10). This, for him, is practical holiness!

Pure here means sincere. Paul uses a compound word which carries the ideas of judgment and the light of the sun. You notice a sweater, or a skirt in a department store; but under the artificial light it is hard to tell exactly what the shade is. 'May I look at this outside?' you ask. You take it outside and hold it up in the daylight to see what the real colour is. That is the kind of purity that God begins to work into the lives of his people: we live in such a way that the truth about us is clear. We belong to Christ; we want to be holy. People know where they are with us.

Blameless (v. 10) may mean either that we have not stumbled morally, or that we have not been a cause of stumbling to others. When we grow in love and discernment both become true. We learn to see temptation and sin in their true light, and to turn away from them. But we also learn to live with a loving concern for others, sensitive to their weaknesses and temptations. Like Paul, we make up our minds that we will not put a stumbling block in the way of our fellow-Christians (*Rom.* 14:13; cf. *1 Cor.* 8:9–13). Mature Christians have learned the difference between what is legitimate for themselves and what is helpful for others (*1 Cor.* 10:23–24).

Filled with the fruit of righteousness (v. 11) is also an ambiguous expression. Is Paul speaking about righteousness as the fruit of grace, or of a new lifestyle which is the fruit of righteousness? In either case the consequence is the same: a life that is right with God, both in terms of our relationship to him (justification) and our obedience to him (holiness). The one never exists apart from the other.

All this, notice, is *to the glory and praise of God* (v. 11). This is the goal of Paul's prayers; it is also the very reason for our existence. 'What is the chief end of man?' asks the first question of the Westminster Shorter Catechism. Its answer is: 'Man's chief end is to glorify God, and to enjoy him for ever'.

That is the kind of *knowledge and depth of insight* Paul prayed for the Philippians. We need to continue to pray for it, both for ourselves and for each other.

5

To Advance the Gospel

Now I want you to know, brothers, that what has happened to me has really served to advance the gospel. As a result, it has become clear throughout the whole palace guard and to everyone else that I am in chains for Christ. Because of my chains, most of the brothers in the Lord have been encouraged to speak the word of God more courageously and fearlessly (Phil. 1:12–14).

Paul's immense affection for the Christians at Philippi is already evident in the opening verses of this wonderful letter. They were his 'joy and crown' (4:1). But the joy in the apostle's heart is all the more remarkable when we remember the circumstances in which he was writing: he was in prison, 'in chains' as he puts it (v. 7).

It was characteristic of Paul under such circumstances to fix his mind on the purposes of God in his life rather than on his immediate confinement. As he did so, several things lifted his spirits. One, obviously, was the care of his fellow-Christians. The Philippians had sent Epaphroditus to encourage him and minister to him (2:30). They were genuinely concerned about his welfare (4:10). He in turn was equally concerned about the Philippians. He did not want them to be over-anxious about him!

There is something Christ-like in Paul's attitude here. One of the impressive things about Jesus' ministry to his disciples in the last hours of his life was that, despite his own need, he was concerned to comfort and strengthen them. John tells us that although our Lord was deeply troubled (*John* 13:21), he encouraged the disciples not to be troubled (*John* 14:1). The language in both verses is the same, which is probably John's way of inviting us to link these two verses together.

Like Jesus, Paul was more concerned about others (in this case, the Philippians) than about his own comfort. He practised what he preached (cf. 2:4). But more than that, he knew that God invariably means to bring new blessings out of the trials and difficulties his servants experience. In these verses he mentions several ways in which this was actually happening.

THE ADVANCE OF THE GOSPEL

Paul was a prisoner of the Roman authorities. From a human point of view his freedom had been curbed and therefore his evangelistic mission seemed to be at an end. But in fact, as he now realised, his imprisonment was part of the divine strategy to advance the gospel by bringing it to people who otherwise would never hear it.

The Roman soldiers who guarded Paul were unlikely to seek out where this despised wandering preacher would next proclaim the gospel. How, then, could the good news about Christ break into the world of the Roman army? Only if Paul were to have extended periods in the company of Roman soldiers! Prison was the ideal setting for such an evangelistic outreach! And so, if imprisonment was the prerequisite for mission, a prisoner Paul would become.

Was there one particular family whose faces broke into smiles when this part of the letter was read out in the church meeting? The Philippians, of all people, knew that God did unexpected things in prisons (*Acts* 16:22–34). They knew that when a Christian such as Paul places his life at the disposal of Christ no circumstances can ever prove to be a final barrier to the advance of the gospel. God's servants may be imprisoned, but the word of God can never be chained (see *2 Tim.* 2:9).

MANIFESTATION OF CHRIST

As a result of Paul's imprisonment *the whole palace guard* had come to realise that he was *in chains for Christ* (v. 13). These were soldiers of both high quality and long experience. They knew that Paul was different. Soon they learned the reason for his imprisonment: his only crime was loyalty to Christ.

Here was a prisoner who prayed and whose heart was full of joy. Here was a prisoner so deeply loved that people visited him from afar in order to encourage him with messages of affection from his fellow-Christians, and material gifts to meet his personal needs. No doubt it was not long before the talk among the soldiers was 'the only chains that bind this man are the ones by which he is bound to Jesus Christ'.

Paul's own words underline this point. Our translations suggest that Paul wrote that he was *in chains for Christ* (v. 13). That was certainly true. But in fact Paul uses his favourite phrase 'in Christ'. He is a prisoner because of his union with Christ. At least some of these soldiers became conscious that the explanation for this prisoner's life was actually found in Someone Else. Did they become conscious too, while they were guarding him, that this Someone Else was there, in prison with him?

In the Great Commission (*Matt.* 28:18–20) Jesus commanded his disciples to go into all the world with the gospel and promised that he would be with them. Paul was experiencing the fulfilment of that promise in a context where he probably least expected it. But he was also discovering something else: his Master had claimed that 'all authority' belonged to him. He would extend his kingdom by his own sovereign power, in his own perfect wisdom. It was this assurance, that his Saviour reigned, that gave Paul such a glorious sense of usefulness even when, humanly speaking, all usefulness was denied him.

There is surely a vital practical lesson here: We can trust Christ's purposes, even when we do not yet fully understand them (see *John* 13:7).

THE CHURCH ENCOURAGED

Barriers to Paul's ministry had become opportunities for its expansion among the praetorian guard. But there was an unexpected 'bonus', which Paul goes on to record. His experience in prison had encouraged his fellow-Christians to such an extent that they were now sharing the gospel with others *more courageously and fearlessly* (v. 14).

Paul does not explain in detail why his imprisonment had such an impact on his fellow-believers. It has been suggested that the special protection afforded to Paul by his Roman citizenship would have reduced the level of timidity in his fellow-Christians who were also Roman citizens. But the words *encouraged* and *courageously* suggest that this new upsurge of witness was not the result of difficulties being eased for believers. The truth was rather that they were facing up to those difficulties and were now willing to speak for Christ whatever the consequences might be. If personal deprivation (imprisonment) led to fruitful witness for Paul, then they could trust that the Lord could work in the same way in their own lives.

God's logic is very different from ours. We assume that the circumstances must be right if we are to be really effective Christians. But God is not waiting for the circumstances to be right; he is committed to producing really effective Christians, whatever their circumstances may be. Does that teach us something about our own Christian witness, and our own circumstances?

6

Mixed Motives

It is true that some preach Christ out of envy and rivalry, but others out of goodwill. The latter do so in love, knowing that I am put here for the defence of the gospel. The former preach Christ out of selfish ambition, not sincerely, supposing that they can stir up trouble for me while I am in chains. But what does it matter? The important thing is that in every way, whether from false motives or true, Christ is preached. And because of this I rejoice (Phil. 1:15–18a).

Paul's experience during his imprisonment had encouraged many of his fellow-Christians to be bold and courageous in their witness. What at first sight must have seemed to them to be a catastrophe for the church had proved to be a divinely planned opportunity for Paul to bring the gospel to members of the Roman military.

Presumably many of these early Christians now concluded: 'If the Lord is able to work in such circumstances in Paul's life, perhaps he will work similarly in the things I tend to think of as setbacks, obstacles and trials.'

It may have been a temptation for Paul to say no more on the subject. After all, his purpose in sending personal news to the Philippians was to encourage them. Why, then, give them news which might prove discouraging? But the apostle is not like some leaders in the church who feel under obligation to tell their supporters only news of success. He realised that his relationship with the Philippians required honesty and openness. The truth was that mixed motives were involved in the increase of the preaching of Christ.

This is not an easy passage fully to understand, but underlying it are certain clear principles.

THE UGLINESS OF FALSE MOTIVES

Some preach Christ out of envy . . . out of selfish ambition, not sincerely, supposing that they can stir up trouble for me while I am in chains . . . from false motives (1:15, 17, 18).

Our instinctive reaction to these words may be: 'No true Christian would ever dream of behaving in such a way! It is impossible to preach Christ *out of selfish ambition.*' For that reason interpreters have sometimes understood Paul to be speaking of false teachers who were preaching a gospel that was not really a gospel at all (as in Galatians 1:6–9). But Paul could not have rejoiced in that.

It is possible to preach the gospel with false motives, just as it seems to be possible to 'prophesy' and 'drive out demons and perform many miracles' in Jesus' name from false motives (*Matt.* 7:22). Perhaps, for example, some were preaching in the hope that they would be able to usurp Paul's authority and gain positions of influence in the churches in his absence.

Whoever they were, these preachers wanted to *stir up trouble* for Paul while he was in prison (v. 17). The word for *trouble* means friction or pressure. He is saying, 'These men are not content to see me in chains; they want to rub the chains into my flesh.'

How appalling that people had such motives. Indeed; but the past tense is not the only one that is appropriate, surely. We need to search our own hearts lest similar selfish ambition lurks within us.

THE BEAUTY OF TRUE MOTIVES

False motives are always more complex than true ones, and they usually take longer for Paul to describe. Thankfully it seems that many others were preaching Christ from motives of *goodwill* and *love.*

But for whom? Certainly for Paul. After all, this group of Christians had been encouraged in their witness by the apostle's faithfulness. He had shown them the way; without his example they would not have served Christ with the vigour and success they did.

They were grateful to him and anxious to see him experience the blessings they shared. They hoped that their new-found courage would give him fresh encouragement.

In addition, however, the preaching of these faithful Christians would have been marked by goodwill and love towards their hearers. That was in marked contrast to Paul's enemies who were driven by selfish ambition. They were simply using their hearers in order to promote themselves. Rather than being able to say we are 'your servants for Jesus' sake' (*2 Cor.* 4:1) they were making their hearers servants of their own ambition.

It is clear now why Paul prayed for his fellow-believers in Philippi that their 'love might abound more and more in knowledge and depth of insight, so that you . . . may be pure and blameless' (1:10). Jealousy, self-centredness, the desire for position and influence still rear their ugly heads in the context of the Christian church. Here Paul provides us with a test of how deeply this prayer has been answered in our own lives. What lies behind our Christian service? Is it an expression of our love for Christ and for others? Or does it mask a driving determination for self-promotion? Do we have mixed motives? Or has Christ purified them?

THE STRENGTH OF PAUL'S MOTIVES

Paul's response to these frustrating experiences is a model of grace and gives us an insight into the motives which determined his own ministry. He was able to rejoice, despite the fact that people were trying to rub salt into his wounds.

But how could anyone say under these circumstances, *I rejoice* (v. 18)? Answer that question and we will learn an important practical principle for the whole of our Christian lives.

Paul's answer is: *Christ is preached.* Far from rejoicing in the false motives of these men who regarded him as a rival rather than a colleague, he exposed them as the self-absorbed individuals they were. But rather than allow their sin to eat away at his soul, discourage him and potentially introduce a note of cynicism into his life, Paul refused to allow himself to be diverted from the main business of his ministry: exalting the name of his Lord Jesus

Christ. The wrong motives of bad men must never be allowed to become the determining element in our attitude to either our own lives or the fellowship of the saints.

That is often a great snare for Christians who are committed to the truth of the gospel. It is very easy to develop a streak of bitterness in our spirits when we see the errors of other professing Christians. The way in which we present the gospel can then be dominated by our criticism of others rather than by a presentation of Jesus Christ. The result is an unattractive harshness, which does not commend Christ. We learn from Paul that recognising false motives and even errors in others need not produce an un-Christlike temperament. So long as the one concern of our lives is to honour Christ we will be safeguarded.

Motives matter; but we must never allow the motives of others to devour us. We must reserve in our hearts a sanctuary of love for Jesus Christ – a sanctuary from which everything but trust in him and love for him is barred.

7

Reason for Joy

Yes, and I will continue to rejoice, for I know that through your prayers and the help given by the Spirit of Jesus Christ, what has happened to me will turn out for my deliverance. I eagerly expect and hope that I will in no way be ashamed, but will have sufficient courage so that now as always Christ will be exalted in my body, whether by life or by death. For to me, to live is Christ and to die is gain (Phil. 1:18b–21).

P aul rejoiced in the spread of the good news about Jesus Christ despite the jealousy of certain people who viewed him as a rival. He was determined that nothing should invade and destroy the joy in Christ which was his birthright as a Christian. Despite opposition he experienced true joy. But he had other reasons to rejoice as he looked forward.

This further aspect of his joy is based on three things: what he knows, what he anticipates God will do and what Christ means to him. He knows that he will experience *deliverance* (v. 19); he expects that *Christ will be honoured* (v. 20), because his Lord means more to him than everything else (v. 21).

DELIVERANCE

Paul anticipates *deliverance* (v. 19). He uses the New Testament's normal term for salvation. But does he mean release from prison, or final salvation?

Since Paul attributes his deliverance to the prayers of the Philippians and the ongoing work of the Holy Spirit we might assume that he was thinking about being acquitted at his forthcoming trial and subsequently being released from prison. Later in verse 25 he seems to suggest that he expects to continue his ministry into the future.

But on the other hand, the words *turn out for my deliverance* are taken directly from Paul's Greek Old Testament, from Job 13:16. Here Job wants to argue his case with God (*Job* 13:3): 'I will surely defend my ways to his face. Indeed, this will turn out for my deliverance' (*Job* 13:15–16). He is clearly thinking of himself being vindicated before the judgment of God rather than before a human tribunal.

It is possible that Paul actually had both judgments in mind. He is trusting in his Lord to keep him faithful in the short term as he is put on trial before a human tribunal; thus he will be 'blameless' (v. 10) and *in no way ashamed* (v. 20) before the judgment of Rome or the judgment of Christ.

CHRIST EXALTED

Various things seem to have led Paul to believe he would be acquitted and free to continue his ministry (see v. 25). But in any case that is not the most important issue for him. Rather, he gives priority to this: *that now as always Christ will be exalted in my body, whether by life or by death* (v. 20).

How is Christ 'exalted' in our lives? Paul's vocabulary provides us with a word picture. 'Exalted' literally means 'made large'. Whenever it becomes clear that we count Christ greater than ourselves, he is honoured. Paul was here simply following the example of John the Baptist who said of Jesus, 'He must become greater; I must become less' (*John* 3:30).

HELP

We often think of others being dependent on the apostle Paul, but too rarely of his sense of dependence on others for help and encouragement. Yet it is clear from his letters that he was constantly conscious of his own weakness and need. He candidly asks for the prayers of others to assist him in his ministry (e.g., *Rom.*

15:30–32; *Eph.* 6:19). Here he is sure that the Philippians who love him so deeply will have been praying for him constantly.

But for what did the Philippians pray? And for what are we to pray for Christians in times of trial? Paul gives us a clue. He anticipates that he will receive the help of the Holy Spirit. The word *help* (v. 19) was employed outside the Bible in various picturesque ways – for example in medicine for a supporting ligament, or in the theatre for the provision the leader of the chorus made for its members. Surely his friends were praying, 'Father, send your Spirit to give Paul help. Support him in his weakness; provide him with everything he needs to be faithful to your Son.'

Did the Philippians and Paul both know the promise that Jesus had given? 'Whenever you are arrested and brought to trial . . . say whatever is given you at the time, for it is not you speaking, but the Holy Spirit' (*Mark* 13:11). He reserves the best of his gifts for the time of our greatest need; of that Paul was certain.

AMBITION

Paul's situation was serious, potentially life-threatening. He faced life and death issues, as the constant repetition of these ideas in verses twenty to twenty-six makes plain. He was not immune to normal human emotions in that context. He speaks about the need for courage so that he will not be ashamed. He knew only too well that loneliness, intimidation and fear of physical pain might place enormous pressure on him to deny his Master. What is the secret of remaining faithful under such pressures?

Paul knew there was something more important than life. He had hinted at it in verse eighteen. He had made it even more explicit in verse twenty. Now he expresses it in the simplest yet profoundest of statements: *For to me, to live is Christ and to die is gain* (v. 21).

The gain, of course, lies in the fact that Paul's death will usher him into the presence of Christ. He will be 'with Christ, which is better by far' (v. 23). But that future experience gives him joy only because in the present Christ means everything to him: *to live is Christ*.

Later in Philippians the apostle will spell out in greater detail what this involves (see 3:7–11). Even here, however, it clearly implies that Christ is the One in whose presence he lives and whose glory is the motive for everything he does. He realises that part of the reason Christ died for him was that he, Paul, should no longer live for himself but for Christ (*2 Cor.* 5:15).

How can we live like that? Only when, as Paul says to the Corinthians, 'Christ's love *compels* us' (*2 Cor.* 5:15). He uses this verb again in Philippians 1:23 ('I am torn between the two'). It originally meant holding something together so that it would not fall apart; in the New Testament it usually has the meaning of gripping, enclosing, putting pressure on something. We feel the love of Christ gripping us as though he had placed his hand on our shoulder so that we cannot release ourselves. The knowledge the gospel gives us of his amazing love masters us. We confess with Isaac Watts:

> *Were the whole realm of nature mine,*
> *That were a present far too small;*
> *Love so amazing, so Divine,*
> *Demands my soul, my life, my all.*

That does not mean we never think about anyone or anything else; but it does mean that we never think about them without remembering that we belong to Christ. Everything we have, all we are – are his.

Can I say *to me to live is Christ?* Then *to die is gain!*

8

Inclinations and Responsibilities

If I am to go on living in the body, this will mean fruitful labour for me. Yet what shall I choose? I do not know! I am torn between the two: I desire to depart and be with Christ, which is better by far; but it is more necessary for you that I remain in the body. Convinced of this, I know that I will remain, and I will continue with all of you for your progress and joy in the faith, so that through my being with you again your joy in Christ Jesus will overflow on account of me (Phil. 1:22–26).

We have seen already that Paul's whole life was centred on Jesus Christ; his will was submitted to the will of his Master. But serving Jesus Christ does not mean that we become automatons with no wills, preferences, or choices of our own. Growing in holiness does not mean that we become bland people; it means that, like Paul, we bring all our preferences to this touchstone: How will Christ be most clearly exalted in my life?

Paul was not sure what his personal choice was (v. 22). In these verses he considers the question of personal preferences, and in the process gives us some guidelines to follow in our own lives. In particular he compares his natural inclinations with his apostolic responsibilities. Of course that alone will not always answer the question, 'What is God's will?' But it does put decision-making into its proper perspective, and in this instance helps Paul to think about the way ahead, all other things being equal.

Here, then, is a practical principle to follow when we are seeking conscientiously to discern the will of God. Place side-by-side, in columns, the answers to two questions: (i) What are my natural desires, preferences and instincts in this situation? (ii) What responsibilities do I have in terms of my home and family, role in my church, stewardship of my gifts, experience in the past?

Often simply listing the answers to these questions helps Christians to have a clearer sense of God's direction, all other things being equal. Sometimes, as in Paul's case, deep certainty will require a further unfolding of God's providence in our lives. Then, like the apostle, we need to learn the art of contented waiting (*Phil.* 4:11–13).

NATURAL INCLINATION

Paul wanted *to depart* (v. 23). Characteristically he employs a graphic word which could be used of a ship weighing anchor, or soldiers striking camp, or even of someone solving a problem. He looks forward to leaving these shores and 'sailing' for glory, of packing up his 'earthly tent' (*2 Cor.* 5:1) and marching on to the heavenly Zion.

But Paul does not merely want to escape from bodily existence, as though it were the prison Greek philosophers believed that it was ('the body is a tomb' they used to say). In fact the apostle was looking forward to a new, resurrection body (see *1 Cor.* 15:42). He does not contrast mortal bodily existence with the immortality of the soul, but with being *with Christ* (v. 23).

Of course Paul would have been glad to be free from the trials of his ministry. Nobody can read what he says in 2 Corinthians 11:23–29 and doubt that. But there were more important considerations for him than freedom from suffering. He is not choosing death, as though he were rejecting life; he is choosing Christ, whom he loves and whom he believes he will get to know better than ever.

TO BE WITH CHRIST

Dying is gain (v. 21) because it means to *be with Christ* (v. 23). Elsewhere Paul states that it is when the Lord Jesus returns that believers will be 'with Christ' (*1 Thess.* 4:17). But there is no necessary tension between these two statements. In 1 Thessalonians Paul envisages the whole church of God being 'with Christ' following his return and the final resurrection. Here he is thinking of what happens to the individual believer at death.

It has sometimes been suggested that Christians 'sleep' (i.e., are unconscious) between death and the final resurrection. Indeed the New Testament sometimes speaks of death as 'sleep' (e.g., *John* 11:11–13; *1 Cor.* 11:30; 15:20; *1 Thess.* 4:14). But these texts seem to have our bodily existence in view. Physically we 'fall asleep'; but the spirit enters immediately into the presence of Christ (cf. *Luke* 23:39–43). Otherwise it would be difficult to see how Paul could regard *to depart* as *better by far,* since it would mean a state of unconsciousness. No, what is better about dying is that for the believer death is the gateway into the presence of his Lord.

Of course there is much about this that is difficult for us to understand. Our only experience of existence is related to our present physical bodies. Yet we are conscious that we ourselves are more than merely physical bodies. As the Westminster Shorter Catechism puts it: 'The bodies of men after death return to dust, and see corruption; but their souls (which neither die nor sleep) having an immortal subsistence [i.e., power of existence], immediately return to God who gave them.'

What a glorious prospect this is for the Christian: our knowledge and love of Christ in the present life are only preliminary to what awaits us after death. It is this assurance which transforms the Christian's attitude to death. Of course there is much about it that is painful and sad, sometimes deeply distressing. But this cheers our spirits: we are travelling home; we are going to see Jesus Christ!

RESPONSIBILITY

Paul was 'torn' between (i) the joy that lay before him in the presence of Christ, and (ii) the alternative of continuing his life and ministry. What would the second alternative involve? *Fruitful labour* (v. 22), he replies.

These are always the alternatives, for all who can say 'to me, to live is Christ and to die is gain'. Christ is Lord of our lives; they come to an end only in his sovereign will, when his purposes in us and for us have been completed. But if it is his will for us to continue to live, one reason is this: he means to continue to bless us and use us as his servants. We too can say, *this will mean fruitful labour for me* (v. 22).

The need of the churches he had founded seemed to lead Paul to the conviction that it was surely the Lord's will for his life to be spared and for his ministry to continue so that others might make progress in grace and increase in joy (v. 25).

That is a striking insight. If the Lord continues to keep us in this life, he means our lives to encourage others to grow as Christians and to bring joy to them. That is part of the answer to the question, What is my life really for? It helps us to see what is really important in God's perspective. This is a good question to ask ourselves: Does my life encourage others to grow and to rejoice?

Christians who have few gifts, or are weakened by illness, or who have grown frail in old age should pay special attention to Paul's words here. It is all too easy to feel that you are useless, even a burden to others, and to wish 'to be away'. But here is the secret of maintaining a sweet spirit in adversity: I have a glorious prospect before me when I am with Christ. But for the present, that same Christ means to help others through my presence with them. Even although I can do very little 'practically', nevertheless 'to me, to live is Christ'. When other Christians see that, they will be encouraged and cheered on their way. Indeed, there are few richer blessings than being in the presence of someone who obviously lives for Christ. That is Christian service!

In your contact with others have you learned to believe with the apostle Paul that *through my being with you again your joy in Christ Jesus will overflow on account of me* (v. 26)?

9

Keep Standing!

Whatever happens, conduct yourselves in a manner worthy of the gospel of Christ. Then, whether I come and see you or only hear about you in my absence, I will know that you stand firm in one spirit, contending as one man for the faith of the gospel without being frightened in any way by those who oppose you. This is a sign to them that they will be destroyed, but that you will be saved – and that by God. For it has been granted to you on behalf of Christ not only to believe on him, but also to suffer for him, since you are going through the same struggle you saw I had, and now hear that I still have (Phil. 1:27–30).

Paul's purpose in writing this letter was to express his affection and gratitude to his friends for their gift, and also to deal with a number of pastoral burdens he had. In fact the chief reason chapter one is largely taken up with Paul himself is because he wants to relieve the anxieties his friends have about his welfare.

Paul also wants to assure them that despite his circumstances he has been able to continue his ministry and witness. In fact his circumstances have opened a new and unexpected sphere of service (or was 'the palace guard' [v. 14] a prayer-burden on Paul's heart long before he was imprisoned?). Now, however, he draws attention to the concerns he has for the Philippians.

WORTHY CONDUCT

While Paul anticipates release from confinement, he urges his friends to patterns of Christian lifestyle which are not dependent on his own presence or absence. That is a challenging and an important principle. Was there a quality about their Christian commitment when Paul was present which was lacking when he was not with them? That would be an all-too-common Christian frailty. Is our presence at worship and prayer, or our support for the various ministries of our fellowship more dependent on the presence of particular leaders than on our faithfulness to Christ?

Consistent Christian service is based on the principle urged on the Philippians in verse twenty-seven: a manner of life *worthy of the gospel of Christ*. It is a recurring note in Paul's letters (cf. *Eph.* 4:1; *Col.* 1:10; *1 Thess.* 2:2; *2 Thess.* 1:5), but one that is sometimes misunderstood. He does not mean that we earn God's favour, but that our lives should be consistent with the gospel, living illustrations of the gospel's power.

This principle is one of the keys to the message of the Bible: when the grace of God in the gospel touches our lives it produces graciousness. Christ begins to transform us into his likeness.

Paul hints at this when he says *conduct yourselves . . .* (v. 27). Literally he writes 'live as a citizen'. Later he tells us that 'our citizenship is in heaven' (3:20). Here we are alien residents and should be easily recognised by the difference in our speech, the customs in our lives, and the fact that we share certain characteristics with other citizens of heaven. Paul is saying: you belong to a heavenly people, therefore live a heavenly life. Remember who you are, where you have come from and where you belong! (See *1 Pet.* 2:11–12.)

FACING OPPOSITION

Even before the Philippians have time to respond, 'But Paul, you don't understand the opposition we experience here', he tells them that he knows all about it! He knows there are always those who *oppose* the people of God (v. 28). Jesus had made that very clear (*John* 15:18) and it was written into the very heart of Paul's apostleship. Had not Jesus told Ananias 'how much he [Paul] must suffer for my name' (*Acts* 9:16)? No matter how gracious we are in our lifestyle, opposition will come, just as it came to Jesus. The question is not whether we will experience it or not, but how we respond to it.

Here Paul explains two things:

(i)   Christians should not be intimidated (*frightened*, v. 28) by opposition. Outside of the New Testament the same language is used of horses startled into a panic. It is a vivid picture of how we sometimes react: we are surprised by any painful trial, despite the New Testament's teaching (cf. *1 Pet.* 4:12). We panic, and we tend to be overcome.

(ii)   Christians do not need to be overcome by such opposition. How? By recognising it for what it is: a twofold sign.

On the one hand it is the mark of destruction on those who oppose us (v. 28). It is not a sign of their greatness and superiority – although they often think it is.

What does Paul mean? Perhaps he remembered the struggles of the psalmist Asaph. He saw the prosperity of men and women who opposed God. They seemed to escape trial and suffering and grow rich. Almost in despair of making sense of this, Asaph went into the temple. There, in the presence of the God of infinite glory and majesty, the Righteous Judge of all the earth, he had a glimpse of their final destiny. He saw that the mark of destruction was on their lives: their feet were on a slippery slope. He was no longer sent into a panic by their opposition. In fact, he saw that their condition was pitiful rather than intimidating (*Psa.* 73:2–20).

But the opposition created by our humble Christian witness can have another effect – of encouraging us! How? It is a sign that we will be saved, says Paul (v. 28). If we are opposed for the sake of Christ (v. 29), it is because we belong to him (*Matt.* 5:11). The opposition that might otherwise discourage us actually serves to assure us that we are truly Christ's. It means that his grace has been seen in our lives! So we remain undaunted by opposition. Encouraged by the fact that Christ is using us, we develop stickability in our Christian witness!

UNWELCOME GIFT?

Paul has a further striking insight to add. The Philippians knew that their faith in Christ was a gift. Of course they were the ones who believed (God does not believe for us). But the object of our faith, Jesus Christ, is God's gift to us. In addition we are brought to faith only through the ministry of the Spirit in our lives. It is, in this sense, *granted* to us. 'But,' Paul now adds, 'don't you see that in a similar way your suffering is a gift?' Of course you suffer. But your suffering is part of God's providence in your life; he is working out his purpose through it. For in his plan, suffering leads to glory and helps to create it (*Rom.* 8:17). Suffering is the friction which polishes our graces. Without it we would be all the poorer as reflectors of the image of his Son.

Suffering tends to isolate people. Those who comfort others do not share in their suffering. But that is not so when Christians suffer. For although our suffering is uniquely ours, we are not alone in it. The Philippians saw Paul *going through the same struggle*. They could see in him, as well as in one another, that through suffering Christ created character (*Rom.* 5:2b–4). That is one of the greatest of all the privileges we enjoy in Christian fellowship: seeing brothers and sisters, often older and wiser, whose graces shine because of all they have been through.

Apparently God is prepared to go to any lengths to make us more like his Son. The cross proves that. We can be sure he will stop at nothing to change us. Suffering is but one of his instruments.

10

Secrets of Unity

*If you have any encouragement from being united with Christ,
if any comfort from his love, if any fellowship with the Spirit, if
any tenderness and compassion, then make my joy complete by
being like-minded, having the same love, being one in spirit and
purpose. Do nothing out of selfish ambition or vain conceit,
but in humility consider others better than yourselves. Each of
you should look not only to your own interests, but also to the
interests of others* (Phil. 2:1–4).

Paul has been exhorting the Philippians to 'stand firm in one
spirit . . . contending as one man' for the gospel (1:27). Unity
in our fellowships is essential to our witness, as Jesus' 'high
priestly' prayer for his people makes clear (*John* 17:21).

There are several reasons for that. One is that the gospel is
a message of reconciliation and peace with God. How can non-
Christians be convinced that Christ reconciles us to God if we are
not reconciled to each other? Another is that disunity always has
the effect of turning a Christian fellowship in on itself, wasting
energy on itself. When we devour ourselves in that way we have
little energy left to be shining light and preserving salt in a needy
world (*Matt.* 5:14–16).

Now Paul turns the spotlight even more directly on the fellowship at Philippi. In the gentlest possible way he hints that he knows
that there are frictions and tensions among them. Later, as we shall
see, he is more specific and even singles out two individuals for
special mention (4:2ff).

In these opening verses of chapter two he shows us how unity is
based on humility (vv. 1–4), then in the famous section that follows

he sets before us a magnificent portrait of Christ as the source and model of true humility (vv. 5–11).

When we see failures in a Christian or a fellowship our natural tendency is either to be critical or simply to demand improvement. Paul's response is wiser and deeper. He recognises that only through grace are we able to change and develop a pattern of transformed attitudes and actions. So he constantly appeals to the privileges of grace before urging us to the obedience of faith. This is obvious in the present passage. Paul argues: if these things are true, then here are the implications that follow.

PAUL'S 'IFS'

Verse one contains four 'ifs'. Paul is not doubting whether the Philippians have any experience of the various things he mentions; in this context 'if' really means 'since'. His logic is as follows: because these Christians have experienced so much blessing, they ought to exhibit the effects of grace in their lives.

But what are these blessings to which Paul appeals?

(i) *Being united with Christ*. Has it never dawned on them what that means? 'In Christ', as we have seen, is Paul's favourite summary expression for all that it means to be a Christian. To be in Christ is to share in all of the blessings he has gained for us. It means to have been chosen in Christ before time began (*Eph.* 1:3–4); to have died to the reign of sin and to be raised into a new life of consecration (*Rom.* 6:2–4, 6–7). It means sharing in a new creation altogether in which all things become new (*2 Cor.* 5:17).

(ii) *Comfort from his love*. Although Paul expresses himself generally here, the NIV understands this as a reference specifically to Christ's love. Had they not felt the grip of Jesus' love for them? He had died for them! Did they not experience what Paul did? 'Christ's love compels us, because we are convinced that one died for all' (*2 Cor.* 5:14).

(iii) *Fellowship with the Spirit*. We are bound to Christ through the gift of the Spirit. There is only one Holy Spirit. The Spirit who dwelt on our Lord also dwells in our hearts. The same Spirit dwells in all of our fellow-believers! We are one with them in the fellowship of the Spirit.

(iv) *Tenderness and compassion.* If this too is a reference to our Lord it reminds us that he is 'gentle and humble' (*Matt.* 11:29); he possesses 'meekness and gentleness' (*2 Cor.* 10:1). He does not break bruised reeds or extinguish smouldering wicks (*Matt.* 12:20; cf. *Isa.* 42:3).

If we belong to his family it follows that these will be the family characteristics produced in us. Have we not experienced that in relationship to our fellow-Christians?

PAUL'S 'THENS'

Such privileges bring responsibilities. *If* these things are true, *then* certain implications follow. *If* we have received all these blessings in Christ and from Christ, *then* we are responsible to live to Christ and for Christ.

In this context, Paul spells out that this means being willing to put others first in several important ways.

(i) The joy of others. Paul exhorts them to one mind, one love, one spirit, one purpose. That alone is consistent with their new life in Christ. But it will also bring joy to Paul himself.

Make my joy complete he says (v. 2). In the most gentle of ways he is challenging them: Which is more important – your self-indulgence, or giving me – who brought the gospel to you – the joy of seeing you live mature and gracious Christian lives? At the very lowest level, our failures bring sorrow to those who first pointed us to Christ.

'Super-spirituality' responds, in superior fashion: 'My only concern is to give joy to Christ, not to other people.' But it is only as Christ sees us bringing blessing to the lives of others that he rejoices (cf. *John* 15:11).

Here, then, is one (but not the only) test for our motives and actions: Will this bring joy to those who care for me spiritually?

That may give us wise direction when we are uncertain what to do; and in times of spiritual selfishness it will jolt us out of our lethargy.

(ii) Unity with others. Paul also summons them to be *like-minded . . . the same love . . . one in spirit and purpose* (v. 2). This plea is particularly interesting because the Philippians were obviously a deeply committed group of Christians. But sometimes those who have deep commitment to the truth develop a short-sightedness about the nature of truth. They assume that to live in the truth, as the New Testament urges us to do, is only a matter of right doctrine. But to live in the truth means more than having our theology right. It means embodying its implications in lives of graciousness and humility.

Where there is only superficial commitment to the gospel there is little risk of serious division. Why divide over relatively un-important issues? But where there is zeal, that danger always exists if the zeal is not permeated with humility. Perhaps more disunity is caused in the church by a lack of humility than by a lack of zeal.

Are we working towards this unity of mind, love, spirit and purpose?

(iii) The value of others. What value do you place on others? Here is the secret of a genuinely united Christian fellowship: its members count each other more important than themselves (v. 3). Here *better* does not mean that we should engage in a charade, ignoring others' faults. No, Paul is telling us that we should count each member of our fellowship more important than ourselves. We have the strongest possible motive for doing this: Christ counted our salvation more important than preserving his own life. In Christ we are to become like him.

Notice the alternative. It is not merely being a mediocre Christian. It is *selfish ambition* and *vain conceit*. The alternative to valuing others for Christ's sake is to become spiritually disfigured ourselves.

In the ancient world in general, and in a society like Philippi in particular, a Roman colony with its well-ordered social scale and values, *humility* (literally 'humble-mindedness') was not a highly-esteemed grace. But to display it is to replace the value system of

this world with the values of heaven. We are never more like Christ
than when we live like that.

Thus, Paul says, we should be concerned about the interests and
concerns of others not merely our own. In the verses that follow he
not only gives us the greatest example of such humble love in the
Son of God. He goes on to point out that the Philippians have seen
it in two men they know well.

How sad if we should claim to have received all these privileges
– *united with Christ, the incentive of love, fellowship with the Spirit,
tenderness and compassion* – and yet bear none of their fruits!

II

The Attitude of Christ

Your attitude should be the same as that of Christ Jesus:
Who, being in very nature God,
   did not consider equality with God
     something to be grasped,
but made himself nothing,
   taking the very nature of a servant,
   being made in human likeness.
And being found in appearance as a man,
   he humbled himself
   and became obedient to death – even death on a cross!
                      (Phil. 2:5–8).

When Augustine was asked to list the central principles of the Christian life he replied, 'First, humility; second, humility; third, humility.' This is the theme Paul is now pursuing. His great concern at this juncture is that the Philippians should 'stand firm in one spirit, contending as one man for the faith of the gospel' (1:27). But, as we have seen, that requires a genuine unity among Christians which, according to Paul, depends on humility.

The verses which follow constitute one of the great New Testament passages on the person and work of Christ. In a piece of magnificent exposition Paul expounds the humility and the exaltation of the Son of God.

Perhaps no passage in the New Testament has attracted the interest of scholars so much as this one. Its poetic grandeur has raised the question of its origin: is it an early Christian hymn? It is easy to see from the way the NIV sets out verses six to eleven that the wording may have been derived from a hymn of six three-line verses (the words *even death on a cross!* in verse eight possibly being added by Paul). If these verses were taken from an early hymn, who wrote it? Paul? Or someone else? We cannot be sure. More important by far are the statements these verses make about the identity of Christ.

In particular, we need to notice why Paul uses them. He explains in verse five, which literally reads: 'Think among you that which [you] also [think] in Christ Jesus.' This may mean: 'Imitate the thinking of Christ', or, alternatively: 'Develop this mind-set in your fellowship, which is the only consistent mind-set for those who are in Christ Jesus.'

The second interpretation is probably the better one. But in either case, since he goes on to expound the humble-mindedness of Christ, Paul is urging us to live out our fellowship with our humble Saviour in practical ways in our lives. To be proud is to act out of character for those who are Christ's. To be humble-minded is to be our truest selves in him.

Here again Paul points us to the basic framework for Christian living. Over and over again in his letters he employs a basic formula which he fleshes out in many different ways: we are in Christ; we are, therefore, to become more and more like Christ. The imitation of Christ is not an activity we engage in out of our own resources, but depending on the graces of Christ himself.

THE SELF-HUMBLING OF THE LORD

The greatness of our Lord's self-humbling is measured by how low he was prepared to stoop from the great heights which were his natural and rightful environment. He was *in very nature God* (v. 6), or 'in the form of God'. It is clear from the next line that Paul meant this in the sense that Christ possessed *equality with God.* The Son did not 'grasp' or jealously guard his rights as Son of God. Instead he was willing to come to our fallen, helpless world on our behalf. He was under no obligation to do so.

Yet Jesus *made himself nothing* (v. 7), or 'emptied himself'. Paul does not mean that he evacuated himself of the power of deity. He explains that his words mean that Jesus took *the very nature of a servant, being made in human likeness.* Lord of glory though he was, he emptied himself not by subtraction of his divine attributes but by the assumption of human nature. He was Immanuel, God truly with us, fully God and yet truly man.

Then there took place a second stage in this amazing humbling: as the servant of God he *became obedient* to his Father, even to the extent of dying *on a cross* in naked shame as a condemned criminal. That any good man should be willing to humble himself in this way for the blessing of others is breathtaking; that the Offended One, the Lord of glory should willingly enter into such humiliation should bring awed adoration to our hearts.

Several expressions Paul uses help to illuminate the wonder of Christ's grace. They suggest, as it might be put, that Jesus is portrayed here as 'Adam in reverse' (cf. *Rom.* 5:12–21).

(i) *Being in very nature God* he *did not consider equality with God something to be grasped* (v. 6) reminds us of Adam's failure. He was created as the image and likeness of God (*Gen.* 1:26). But he *grasped* after equality with God ('you shall be as God' [*Gen.* 3:5] the tempter suggested). By contrast, Jesus, whose right equality with God always was, did not refuse to become *obedient* (v. 8).

(ii) The Son *made himself nothing* [emptied himself] . . . *taking the form of a servant* (v. 7). Here we may have an echo of the great prophecy in Isaiah 52:13–53:12, where the Sufferer 'poured out his life unto death' (*Isa.* 53:12). He is described by God as 'my servant' (*Isa.* 52:12). He did what Adam refused to do: serve God.

(iii) The incarnate Son *became obedient to death.* In Romans 5:12–21 Paul gives us an exposition of these words by means of an extended comparison between Jesus and Adam. Adam's dis-obedience brought sin and death into the world; by contrast, Jesus' obedience brings righteousness and life into it.

The Son of God came to undo the disobedience of Adam and to experience the judgment of God which Adam brought crashing down on the human race. To do so he had to become obedient to his Father's will and plan. This he was throughout the whole of his life, from the cradle to the cross. Even when, in the Garden of

Gethsemane, every natural human instinct in him shrank back from the climactic act of obedience on Calvary, he bowed before his Father and prayed, 'yet not my will, but yours be done' (*Luke* 22:42).

So a twofold contrast lies hidden in Paul's description of Jesus' self-humbling. The contrast between who he is by nature and the identity he has taken on by grace; the contrast between what the Last Adam became and what the First Adam had been. No wonder such theology produced poetry!

We have seen that these verses illustrate a great principle of Pauline theology: union with Christ should lead to the imitation of Christ. Consider what Christ-like humility means: not standing on our so-called rights, but being willing to give them up for the sake of others.

What Paul describes here in the language of theology, John's Gospel portrays graphically in Jesus' humble washing of his disciples' feet in the Upper Room:

Jesus knew that the Father had put all things under his power	*Who, being in very nature God, he did not consider equality with God something to be grasped*
he got up from the meal, took off his outer clothing	*made himself nothing*
he wrapped a towel around his waist . . . and began to wash his disciples' feet. (*John* 13:3–5)	*Taking the form of a servant . . . he humbled himself . . . to . . . death on a cross.* (*Phil.* 2:6–8)

'Now that I, your Lord and Teacher, have washed your feet, you also should wash one another's feet. I have set you an example that you should do as I have done for you' (*John* 13:14–15).

Let each of us look not only to our own interests but also to the interests of others (*Phil.* 2:4)!

12

Name Above Every Name

Therefore God exalted him to the highest place
  and gave him the name that is above every name,
that at the name of Jesus every knee should bow,
  in heaven and on earth and under the earth,
and every tongue confess that Jesus Christ is Lord,
  to the glory of God the Father (Phil. 2:9–11).

Paul moves from his description of the humbling of the Son of God – making himself nothing, taking the nature of a servant, becoming obedient to death – to a magnificent description of Jesus' exaltation.

We have already noticed the parallel between Paul's description in Philippians 2 of our Lord's humble-mindedness and the account of his humble action in washing the feet of his disciples in *John* 13. But the parallel does not stop there:

When he had finished washing	*God exalted him*
their feet, he put on his clothes	*to the*
and returned to his place	*highest place*
(*John* 13:12)	(*Phil.* 2:9)

In the Upper Room Jesus returned to the head of the table in an acted parable of his exaltation. So, in reality, he was welcomed home to the right hand of the Father. God has *exalted him to the highest place* and given to him *the name that is above every name* (v. 9).

The *highest place* is, of course, the place of special honour; but what is *the name that is above every other name?* Since Paul goes on to speak about the whole creation bowing before Jesus as *Lord*, it is

[46]

usually argued that it is this name that Paul has in view. But it may be closer to the truth to suggest that Paul is thinking of the meaning of Jesus' name 'Saviour', combined with the title 'Lord'. For lying behind these verses we can detect the shadow of Isaiah's prophecy:

> Truly you are a God who hides himself,
> O God and Saviour of Israel . . .
>
> I am the Lord,
> and there is no other . . .
>
> And there is no God apart from me,
> a righteous God and a Saviour;
> there is none but me . . .
>
> Before me every knee will bow;
> by me every tongue will swear.
> (*Isa.* 45:15, 18, 21, 23).

Paul is saying that Jesus has been publicly *exalted* to the position which was his before his humiliation. In the flesh through which he identified himself with us, his glory and majesty were normally hidden (*Isa.* 45:15). Now, exalted at the right hand of the Father, his true identity is clear, his eternal majesty is revealed. God is the only Saviour; but Jesus is that Saviour! To the Lord alone *every knee should bow and every tongue confess;* but Jesus is that Lord!

CHRIST'S DEITY

There are few more impressive expositions of Jesus' identity than Paul gives us in these three verses.

(i)   He employs an Old Testament passage in which God as speaker gives a description of himself which applies exclusively to himself. Paul now applies that description to Jesus.

(ii)   He calls Jesus *Lord*. The Greek word is *Kurios*. It appears over six thousand times in the Greek translation of the Old Testament which Paul used (called the Septuagint). In the vast majority of these references the word translates the sacred Hebrew divine name *Yahweh*. Say *Kurios* to a Greek-speaking reader of the Old Testament and he immediately would think of the holy name of the covenant God, *Yahweh*. For Paul, to say that *Jesus Christ is Lord* is not primarily to make a statement about his personal consecration, but about his Saviour's divine identity.

(iii) Paul says that the exaltation of Jesus to heaven's highest place is *to the glory of God the Father* (v. 11). In other words, Jesus' exaltation, and our recognition of it please God. The Lord who brooks no rivals to his divine throne (think what happened when Adam and Eve thought they could be 'equal with God') rejoices in the divine glory of Christ. Why? Paul has already given us the answer: our Lord 'was in very nature God'; equality with God is his eternal right.

We could not ask for a clearer or richer statement of the deity of Christ.

But there is another penetrating implication of this teaching. If the Father exalts Jesus *to the highest place*, he will find any lesser honour being accorded to his Son to be intolerable. Here, then, is one way in which we can recognise those whose hearts are really in tune with God's: what do they make of Jesus? If we do not desire to see him honoured then we are at odds with the Father; the reality of our faith in his Son is very much in doubt.

It is an interesting sidelight on this passage that Jesus Christ now occupies the position of divine honour and glory in heaven. The apostle John gives us some wonderful word-and-symbol portraits of that in Revelation (e.g., chapters 4–5) when he describes Christ at the centre of the throne of God crowned with glory and honour. That is what heaven is like.

When asked, most of us will say 'of course I want to go to heaven'. But do we, if that is what heaven is really like – all the attention and praise being Christ's? If we do not want that in the here-and-now is it likely that we will want it there-and-then?

CONNECTING LINK

There is so much rich teaching in this chapter that we can sometimes ignore the presence of the significant word with which it opens: '*Therefore* . . '. It implies that there is an integral connection between the humiliation of Jesus and his exaltation by the Father.

Whenever we see the word 'therefore' in Paul's letters we should stop to work out the logical connection between what has preceded and what follows. What is it here? It is manifold.

(i)   The exaltation of Jesus fulfils prophecy. We have noticed already that behind Philippians 2:5–11 lies the shadow of the prophecy of the Suffering Servant in Isaiah 52:13–53:12. That prophecy began with this promise: 'See, my servant . . . will be raised and lifted up and highly exalted' (*Isa.* 53:12). Again, in the Messianic prophecy of Psalm 2, the Father is heard promising his Son: 'Ask of me, and I will make the nations your inheritance, the ends of the earth your possession' (*Psa.* 2:8). The exaltation and world-wide recognition of Jesus follows his humiliation simply because his Father promised it would.

(ii)   But that exaltation is also the right of the Son, because he is himself God. As the ancient church's theologians wisely saw, the Bible teaches that the Son is one with the Father in everything except the properties which distinguish him as the Son. He is altogether equal with God, as Paul has indicated in Philippians 2:6. His exaltation is necessary because of his divine identity.

(iii) His exaltation is a logical consequence of his humiliation for a third reason: he is the dear Son of his Father. His Father loves him; his Father has watched him go to the cross; his Father has made him to be sin for us (*2 Cor.* 5:21), and heard him cry 'My God, I am forsaken; why?' But the Father has also heard his earlier prayer: 'Father . . . glorify your Son . . . glorify me in your presence with the glory I had with you before the world began' (*John* 17:1, 5). The love of his Father for him made his exaltation the inevitable consequence of his humiliation.

This is what the Father wants for his Son. One day that will be clear, when, willingly or unwillingly, *every knee will bow* to him *and every tongue confess that Jesus Christ is Lord*.

The question is: Has Jesus' humiliation for our sake led us to the logical conclusion that our knee should bow to him here and now?

But Paul has in mind a particular application of his teaching to the church fellowship at Philippi. Has all that Christ has done and become made any significant impact on their lives? Has it made them humble-minded? That is the only way in which true exaltation becomes possible. Only what goes down will go up!

13

Working out Salvation

Therefore, my dear friends, as you have always obeyed – not only in my presence, but now much more in my absence – continue to work out your salvation with fear and trembling, for it is God who works in you to will and to act according to his good purpose (Phil. 2:12–13).

We have already noticed the importance of the word 'therefore' in Paul's writings in the way in which he connects the exaltation of Christ with his humiliation (2:9). His glory is the logical result of his suffering.

Now we find Paul pointing out that there is a logical connection between the work of Christ and the life of the Christian. Christ obeyed. He was obedient to his Father even although that meant going to the cross. Paul underlines the obvious implication: those who are in Christ and belong to him must also be obedient (2:12).

No Christian ever reaches perfection in this life. Paul, for one, failed to do so, although he continued to grow in grace (3:12). He did not trivialise disobedience. For the apostle, for a professing Christian to live in persistent and habitual disobedience was not merely a sign of immaturity; it was an absurdity. For how can those who belong to the obedient Saviour sit lightly to obedience themselves? It is unthinkable. The inner logic of the gospel makes it impossible for a true Christian to live as though he were 'worldly' (or carnal, *1 Cor.* 3:1).

In addition, Paul scratches beneath the veneer of obedience under which we may be tempted to hide from the scrutiny of the

Spirit of holiness. He urges the Philippians to be just as obedient when he is absent as they are when he is present (v. 12). From what he goes on to say in verses twelve and thirteen it seems clear that he is thinking about their obedience to God, not merely to himself as an apostle (although obedience to God in practice involves obeying the apostolic teaching).

OBEDIENCE – GENUINE OR SUPERFICIAL

Dare we face up to the embarrassing truth that Paul's words suggest? Professing Christians are sometimes obedient only as those who please men rather than those who please God. When an apostle was present, some of the Philippians were 'present and correct'. But perhaps not otherwise.

Are we models of faithfulness in order to please those who lead us, and perhaps ingratiate ourselves with them? Does our zeal falter when they are absent? Do we display different degrees of obedience depending on the identity of our leaders or the public nature of the service we share with them?

What a subtle temptation this is, and how clearly Paul recognised it! That is why he urged the Philippians to be obedient *much more in my absence* (v. 12). He realised that leaders are given to the Christian fellowship in order to encourage obedience. He is not condemning as necessarily superficial obedience which arises because of the presence and ministry of leaders. After all, they are given to us to encourage our obedience. But since that is the case, a greater striving for obedience will be necessary when those leaders are absent and their personal encouragement is withdrawn.

Paul had already spoken to them about this (1:27); now he underlines its importance. There is both spiritual penetration and biblical balance in what he says.

But in what way are the Philippians to show this obedience? By working out their *salvation with fear and trembling* (v. 13).

WORKING IT OUT

Students of Paul's writings have often been puzzled by these words. After all, Paul normally sets 'works' and 'working' over against salvation by grace through Christ. We are not justified by works but by grace. Is he contradicting himself here by saying that salvation is something for which we have to *work?*

Paul is not thinking here of any 'good works' we may contribute to our salvation, but about how we are to respond to the salvation which is ours already in Christ. We are not to work *for* it or work it *up* but work it *out,* that is, to make sure that its influence and implications permeate the whole of our lives. That is well expressed by the NIV translation, *continue to work out your salvation.* It is a lifelong process of obedience in which we see the significance of what Christ has done for us in the ever-changing and developing context of our lives.

It is often suggested that what Paul has in view here is not so much personal *salvation* but the spiritual well-being of the Christian community. No doubt that is an aspect of what he is saying. He is speaking in the context of possible divisions among the Philippians, and urging them to unity (1:27; 2:2; 3:2). But we have already seen that the secret of the unity of a Christian fellowship is our humility and holiness as individuals. We cannot grow as a church unless we grow individually. We cannot work out the implications of salvation into our congregational life unless we are each prepared to see its effects in our personal lives.

How, then, does this happen? Paul's words draw our attention to three elements:

(i) *Salvation has to be worked out.* It is, of course, a free gift; those who receive it are *God's* workmanship (see *Eph.* 2:8–10). But ultimately salvation means the transformation of our lives into the likeness of Christ (cf. *Rom.* 8:29). This implies that, like Christ, we become obedient, we bear the fruit of the Spirit. Salvation does not take place over our heads, as it were, but in our thinking, willing, feeling and doing. The fact that we are in a right relationship with God demands that we live out the practical implications of that relationship.

Paul uses a complex verb here which means not 'work up' but 'work in' your salvation. In this context it may be meant to express the idea of working at something until it is finished or ready. He wants to see salvation transforming every aspect of our lives. This is what it means to be 'saved'. God's grace does not destroy the individual Christian's responsibility to be obedient; rather it makes it possible for that obedience to become a reality in every area of life.

(ii) *The outworking of salvation must be done in fear and trembling.* The phrase is a distinctively Pauline one (see *1 Cor.* 2:3; *2 Cor.* 7:15; *Eph.* 6:5. Cf. *Psa.* 2:11).

It might at first sight seem that in these passages this attitude is related to other people. But a closer examination suggests that, whatever the human context, Paul is thinking of the way in which the Christian should always be conscious that he or she lives before the face of God. There should always be a sense of awe in the life of the believer; a sense of living where we are always visible, always understood through and through, and – amazingly – always loved by the Holy One.

This sense of awe produces a special quality in our obedience; it gives it direction (we are not to be men-pleasers, but God-honouring); it gives it integrity (our obedience is tested by a more discerning eye than those of our fellow-sinners); it is an obedience suffused with humility in which self-projection has given way to devotion to the Lord.

(iii) *Working out our salvation is a high calling.* But Paul does not throw us back on our own resources. We are to work out our salvation, not only because God has worked it into us by his grace, but because he continues to work it out in our lives! He is constantly at work in us so that we have both the will and the power to do what pleases him!

In these verses Paul protects us from two very common errors in thinking which lead in turn to errors in living. We are prone to think either:

(i) If I am to work hard in relationship to salvation then I contribute my part to it, *or*

(ii) If God works in me, then I do not need to work hard at following Christ.

But this is not Paul's logic. He teaches as follows:

Our *salvation* is God's gift.

God's gift summons us to *work out* that salvation into every part of our lives.

We are to work out salvation into our lives in the confidence that *God* is always at work in us to achieve that goal.

Understand this, and we will receive both the challenge and the encouragement of these verses to pursue the holiness without which none of us will see the Lord (*Heb.* 12:14).

14

Let Your Light Shine

*Do everything without complaining or arguing, so that you may
become blameless and pure, children of God without fault in a
crooked and depraved generation, in which you shine like stars in
the universe as you hold out the word of life – in order that I
may boast on the day of Christ that I did not run or labour for
nothing. But even if I am being poured out like a drink offering
on the sacrifice and service coming from your faith, I am glad
and rejoice with all of you. So you too should be glad and rejoice
with me* (Phil. 2:14–18).

Paul has been encouraging the Philippians to wholehearted
commitment to Christ and to letting the implications of their
salvation deeply affect every aspect of their lives. The most basic
reason for doing so is: this is what God is working in them for. In
the past he began the good work of salvation in them; in the future
he will bring it to completion (1:6); in the present he is pursuing it
with vigour!

Now Paul moves from the general principle to a specific illustration, one which is particularly relevant to the Philippians. If the
God of grace and peace is at work in their lives to give them the
ability to will and to do what pleases him, certain things follow.
Paul states them first negatively and then positively.

NEGATIVES

The Philippians are called to *do everything without complaining or
arguing* (v. 14).

Paul frequently saw important parallels between the experiences of the people of God in the events of the exodus and the life of the New Testament church. The language here suggests that the events described in Deuteronomy 31 and 32 were in his mind as he thought of the Philippians. There Moses was speaking about the behaviour of the people while he was present with them, and his fears for them when he would be absent from them after his death (31:26–29). He goes on in Deuteronomy 32:5 to use the language which Paul later employs in Philippians 2:15.

In verse fourteen, however, Paul is thinking of the sin of the people of Israel when, only six weeks out of Egypt, they began to murmur about their provisions and to grumble against Moses and Aaron.

Why was this such unacceptable behaviour? Because it was deep ingratitude in the face of the saving grace and continuing activity of God. A *complaining or arguing* spirit is an expression of ingratitude to God's providence and of lovelessness and pride towards others. It is a denial of grace; it is working against salvation rather than working salvation out into every aspect of our lives. In the face of the self-humbling of Jesus and the servant-spirit which was his, murmuring and argument are ugly monsters. Every child of God should recognise instinctively that they are what Americans call 'no–no's'.

Parents feel very responsible to make sure their children realise that there are 'no–no's'. What about our own lives as children of the living God?

But we cannot live healthy lives only on the basis of negatives. That is a trap Christians have too often fallen into, but it is one that Paul always carefully avoided. His teaching on putting away specific sinful patterns of life is always joined to exhortations to develop Christ-like graces. In fact both negative and positive exhortations are rooted in the fact that we are united to Christ and *therefore* have both the resources and the motivation for a new life-style.

POSITIVES

When we see the benefits to be gained by denying self as we follow Christ we realise why that self-denial is so important, and so worthwhile. We are called to be *blameless and pure, children of God* (v. 15). The negatives of the Christian life all have a positive motivation: we are children of the heavenly Father; we therefore turn away from a spirit of complaint and dissatisfaction because it is so out-of-keeping with the spirit of his family.

Those who truly know God know that he is a gracious and open-hearted Father. Our efforts to please him by reflecting his image in our lives are no better than a child's first attempts at drawing a picture of daddy. But he does not chide our lack of artistry; instead he welcomes it and rejoices in it, because it has been done out of love and gratitude for him. Those who murmur and complain betray the ingratitude of what the New Testament calls the 'spirit of bondage', not the fruit of the 'Spirit of sonship' (see *Rom.* 8:15–16).

Christians need to remind themselves many times a day, 'I am a child of the heavenly Father.' Meditate on that blessing and its far-reaching implications. It will change your life; it will sweeten your spirit; it will put a touch of heaven into your soul. Stop now and think about it.

SHINING LIGHTS

Underlying Paul's thinking here is a principle: Christian witness is dependent not merely on what we say but on what we are. How often we deny the truth of the gospel by the spirit in which we speak, or the un-gospel-like tendencies our lives exhibit! But, says the apostle, when we 'work out' the 'salvation' which is ours in union with Christ, and these negatives and positives are in place, our whole life becomes a powerful witness to those around us. We may not be conscious of it; but they cannot ignore it. They will either be drawn to Christ, or will repel him.

We are the light of the world, said Jesus, *the* Light of the world, and we must let that light shine (*Matt.* 5:14–16). Similarly, says Paul, when salvation is worked into our lives we *shine like stars in the universe* as we *hold out the word of life* (vv. 15–16).

Outside of the New Testament the word translated *stars* is sometimes used of navigational beacons. Perhaps Paul is thinking not only of the brightness and beauty of stars set against the dark sky, but of the safety to which they pointed. No doubt Paul the tentmaker had learned a good deal about seamanship on his missionary journeys! Christians are the bright lights in an otherwise dark world; they are the stars by which others may learn to chart a course to the safety which can be found only in Jesus Christ.

As children we learned to say: 'Twinkle, twinkle, little star, How I wonder what you are.' Christians who are lights shining in this world's darkness will make others ask similar questions. You are the light of the world. Shine!

UNEXPECTED MOTIVE

We might be able to anticipate that Paul would urge the Philippians to ongoing commitment to Christ in order that they might be faithful witnesses to their Lord. But here he adds an unexpected additional motive: *In order that I may boast on the day of Christ that I did not run or labour in vain* (v. 16).

Has Paul lost his sense of modesty? Elsewhere he says that before the judgment seat every mouth will be shut; there will be no room for boasting (*Rom.* 3:19, 27). Here, however, he wants to boast on that day, and is encouraging the Philippians to help him!

These words are not those of an egocentric. Paul's *labour* (v. 16, like *run* the term denotes strenuous effort) is the fruit of God's grace (cf. *1 Cor.* 15:10). Since Paul made it his aim to boast in nothing except the cross (*Gal.* 6:14), ultimately what he is boasting in here should be seen as the result of his fellowship with the crucified and risen Christ (cf. *2 Cor.* 10:13; 11:16–12:10).

Perhaps, as in Corinth, Paul's apostolic ministry was being maligned by others. Here he appeals to Christians whom he knows are devoted to him. To their other motives for serving Christ he adds this one: If you love me, live in a way that will enable me to say to our Saviour, 'Lord Jesus, just look at the fruit of grace in the Philippians!'

How could he bring himself to appeal thus to their love for him? Because he was conscious of the depth of his love for them. He refers to the Old Testament practice of pouring out wine to accompany the main sacrifice (e.g., *Num.* 15:3–12). He was prepared to pour out his life-blood *like a drink offering* to complete their sacrificial faith. He loved them; he rejoiced with them in what God had been doing in their lives. It was only natural that they should *rejoice* with him. It would also be a sign that they were truly spiritual (v. 18)!

How about me? Am I prepared to sacrifice myself, in life or even in death, for the sake of my fellow-Christians? Christ was (2:5–11); Paul was (2:17). Am I?

15

Good News, Bad News

*I hope in the Lord Jesus to send Timothy to you soon, that I
also may be cheered when I receive news about you. I have
no-one else like him, who takes a genuine interest in your
welfare. For everyone looks out for his own interests, not those
of Jesus Christ. But you know that Timothy has proved
himself, because as a son with his father he has served with me
in the work of the gospel. I hope, therefore, to send him as soon
as I see how things go with me. And I am confident in the
Lord that I myself will come soon* (Phil. 2:19–24).

'Like cold water to a weary soul is good news from a distant
land' wrote the wise man (*Prov.* 25:25). Paul had been glad
to have news of the Philippians as well as a gift from them. Now
he was responding in kind, sending them word of his current
situation. He wanted his friends to know how God was advancing
the kingdom through his imprisonment (1:13–14) and about his
own prospects for release (1:25).

At first sight this new section seems to pick up the apostle's
account of his missionary work and the personnel who shared in it
with him, particularly Timothy and Epaphroditus, the two men
best known to the church at Philippi. He had begun to digress
from that in 1:26. Now in 2:19–24 he seems to return to it and gives
a brief report on Timothy and in verses 25–30 a similar report on
Epaphroditus.

There is, however, more to these two cameo portraits of Paul's
fellow-servants than this. Having sent Epaphroditus to Paul, the

Philippians may have been hoping that Timothy would be free to come, not only to bring news of Paul but also to minister to them. Paul was certainly anxious himself to have his impressions (v. 19).

Instead, Paul was sending Epaphroditus back to Philippi. That required an explanation, lest the Philippians thought their messenger had somehow failed either them or Paul, or perhaps even both. In 2:25–30 Paul makes it clear that this is not the case. He shows a wonderfully sensitive concern that his friend should not be subject to misunderstanding and criticism.

But the reference to Timothy and Epaphroditus is particularly appropriate at this juncture for another reason. It completes the pattern of teaching in chapter two. Paul has urged the Philippians to be humble (vv. 1–4); he has expounded that pattern from the example of Christ himself (vv. 5–11), and drawn out its implications and the motivations which should encourage it (vv. 12–18). Now he is saying, albeit by means of gentle hints: here are two men you know who illustrate the very qualities you are to imitate. Salvation has been worked out into their characters – look at them and you will know exactly what I mean!

PROVEN SERVICE

There were reasons for sending Epaphroditus back, as we will see in 2:25–30. There was also a reason for *not* sending Timothy at the moment: his proven service. As far as he could read the providence of God in his life, Paul expected that he would be released. But he could not yet be certain what the verdict of Rome would be. Until that was known much remained uncertain. He himself needed fellowship. In addition, if things were to go contrary to his expectation and execution awaited him, there might be much to do and say which would make Timothy's presence essential (as was true later, *2 Tim.* 4:9). In any case, Paul had *no one else like . . . Timothy* [who had] *proved himself, because as a son with his father he has served with me in the work of the gospel* (2:22).

The words *as a son with his father* give us a clue to the relationship between Paul and his friend. It was more than formal; it was instinctive. Later Paul would draw on that in his direct appeal to him to continue to serve Christ faithfully: 'You . . . know all about my teaching, my way of life, my purpose, faith, patience, love, endurance, persecutions, sufferings' (*2 Tim.* 3:10–11). Here the word 'know' is literally 'follow closely'. Timothy had been an eye-witness at close quarters of 'the real Paul'. In the apostle, Jesus Christ had given him not only a mentor but, undoubtedly, his closest and dearest friend (see *2 Tim.* 1:3–4). In turn, Timothy was in a special sense Paul's spiritual son. At such a critical time he needed him, as he would again later in his life (*2 Tim.* 4:9).

This kind of relationship is a common pattern in Scripture (Moses has Joshua; Elijah has Elisha; Peter has Mark). Leaders must prove themselves by serving with others first. It is thus that they learn not only how to lead, but what it is like to be led! Unfortunately some of us want to be leaders but have never allowed ourselves to be led. Whatever leadership gifts we may have, we lack the one thing needful: a servant spirit.

RELIABILITY

Timothy was not without his weaknesses and his personal diffi-culties. Yet it is apparent that Paul had come to feel his younger friend was absolutely reliable. No one else with him exhibited that quality to the same extent (v. 20). For this reason he seems to have used him regularly as his apostolic deputy to other congregations. That was true here; it was also true of the less mature congregation at Thessalonica (*1 Thess.* 3:2–6), and of the difficult congregation at Corinth where Paul's advance notice of his coming contains a none-too-gentle hint that Timothy is to receive their full respect (*1 Cor.* 16:10–11)!

Here was a man whom an apostle could trust. That was the quality that stuck out. You knew where you were with Timothy; his word was his bond; his actions were consistent. There was no danger that he had entered apostolic ministry to increase his own kudos.

This was the good news: there was no one else like Timothy. Sadly, that was also the bad news.

What would the apostle say about us?

SELF-GIVING

What, then, lay at the root of the difference between Timothy and others? *I have no-one else like him who takes a genuine interest in your welfare. For everyone looks out for his own interests, not those* [interests] *of Jesus Christ* (2:20–21).

These words deliberately echo verses 3 and 4 in which Paul had urged the Philippians to look out not only for their own interests, but for each other's. It was in that context that he had introduced the 'attitude' of the Son of God (v. 5). He, supremely, had been concerned for others' interests, not for his own. He 'did not consider equality with God something to be grasped' (2:6). That pattern Paul saw repeated in his spiritual son, Timothy.

The lesson is obvious. The best friends are those who imitate our Lord Jesus in looking out for the interests, needs, and concerns of others. Such have been delivered from the bondage of self-obsession; they are free to live in self-forgetfulness, full of Christ's grace, delighting to be the servants of others.

This was the secret of Paul's own ministry. He was quite clear that he did not preach himself, 'but Jesus Christ as Lord'. Yet he was able to add, 'and ourselves your servants [bondslaves] for Jesus' sake' (*2 Cor.* 4:5). No wonder Paul's ministry bore such rich fruit; it was genuine ministry, true service. He had learned that from his Lord, Jesus Christ. In Paul, Timothy had seen Christ's image expressed. To give himself for the sake of others had become a spiritual instinct in him also.

Does anyone say about you: 'Do you know ———? I know no one like them who is concerned about my interests, and not just their own'?

16

The Risk-Taker

But I think it is necessary to send back to you Epaphroditus, my brother, fellow-worker and fellow-soldier, who is also your messenger, whom you sent to take care of my needs. For he longs for all of you and is distressed because you heard he was ill. Indeed he was ill, and almost died. But God had mercy on him, and not on him only but also on me, to spare me sorrow upon sorrow. Therefore I am all the more eager to send him, so that when you see him again you may be glad and I may have less anxiety. Welcome him in the Lord with great joy, and honour men like him, because he almost died for the work of Christ, risking his life to make up for the help you could not give me (Phil. 2:25–30).

Epaphroditus was the messenger the Philippians had sent to Paul bearing both material gifts and personal encouragement for the apostle (4:18). He had come *to take care of* [Paul's] *needs* (2:25). But in the process Epaphroditus had taken seriously ill and had been *on the point of death* (v. 27).

We have already noted that the Philippians were probably hoping, perhaps even expecting, to see Timothy arrive with news from Paul; the sight of Epaphroditus would in some ways be a disappointment to them. Further, when anyone returns home unexpectedly early from their sphere of Christian service, questions are often asked in whispered tones; knowing comments are made behind their backs. That is the experience of many missionaries today, and it was potentially the case with Epaphroditus too.

Was there a feeling in the early church, as there often seems to be among contemporary Christians, that those who are engaged in so-called full-time service should be immune from the problems others face? Did Paul suspect that some Philippians might feel that Epaphroditus was a spiritual failure? Was he fearful that there might be the occasional snide comment: 'Some people don't seem to be able to handle the pressures and last the pace'? Perhaps he feared for Epaphroditus' good reputation and the future acceptance of his ministry in Philippi.

Paul counters all potential doubt about the quality of his friend's life and service with a glowing report about him. It is full of generous praise; no doubt this modest man blushed with embarrassment when the letter was read out to the gathered congregation. Paul did not spare his friends' blushes when they were in a good and spiritual cause!

There is a lesson for us here. It is all too common when a Christian is mentioned by name to find fellow-Christians distancing themselves from them with critical words and, sadly, sometimes with a harsh and carping spirit. There is all too little generosity of heart in our praise of other Christians. We justify this by stressing the importance of not inflating the ego of a fellow-believer. But the sad truth often is that we are narrow-spirited. We do not count others as more important than ourselves, but are jealous of our own reputation (see 2:3). By contrast, Paul's words are a beautiful reminder of the gratitude and admiration we should have for the graces and gifts of the Spirit in the lives of our fellow-Christians.

QUALITY CONTROL

Epaphroditus was a Christian of sterling quality as the fourfold description of him in verse twenty-five makes clear.

In the fellowship of the apostolic band he had proved to be Paul's *brother*. In him the family likeness to Christ could be seen, as well as the spirit of love and devotion to other members of Christ's family. Furthermore, his commitment to the advance of the gospel was evident; he was a *fellow-worker*, prepared to take his share of the burdens of Christian service.

This interesting description (used again in Romans 16:21 and Colossians 4:11) illuminates Paul's view of Christian experience.

Sometimes a misunderstanding about the exercise of spiritual gifts arises among Christians: if it takes effort it cannot be the fruit of the Spirit's presence. But this is a distortion of the New Testament's teaching. God's grace in our lives does not relieve us of personal activity; it makes us work harder. Paul has already enunciated the general principle: God works in, *therefore* we work out, his grace (2:12–13). We are called to roll up our spiritual sleeves and get down to the business of building the kingdom of God (*1 Pet.* 1:13)!

Epaphroditus is also dignified by the title of *fellow-soldier*. The Christian life is a spiritual war in which believers need to wear the whole armour of God if they are to last through the heat of the battle (*Eph.* 6:10-20). Paul knew that this Philippian Christian could be relied on at such times, just as his own congregation had relied on him to be their faithful apostle (*messenger*) to Paul.

Here, then, was a Christian to be emulated. When we see that the Christian life is fellowship, hard work, spiritual conflict, and service of our fellow-believers, then we are more likely to 'do everything without complaining or arguing' (2:14).

The church at Philippi certainly had had no need to feel ashamed of Epaphroditus when they sent him; they had even less reason to be ashamed of him now that he was returning. His example raises a searching question: Could your church send you on spiritual service without embarrassment?

BURDENED

We tend to avoid doing things that will become a burden to us. Not Epaphroditus. He accepted the onerous task of making what was probably a lengthy journey to visit Paul (assuming the apostle was in Rome it would have taken him several weeks). But he shared the burden of concern which the Philippian church had for their founding apostle (v. 30). En route he had taken *ill, and almost died* (v. 27). His burden for Paul then became Paul's burden for him.

In turn, Epaphroditus had a burdened spirit: *he longs for all of you and is distressed because you heard he was ill* (v. 26). Paul uses language suffused with emotion: Epaphroditus was deeply disturbed and distracted, such was his concern. The vocabulary is reminiscent of the description of Jesus' experience in the Garden of Gethsemane (*Mark* 14:33).

This is what we may experience when we take up the cross and follow Christ. It is not a popular view of the Christian life, for we are too often obsessed instead with what the gospel will do for ourselves (give me peace, purpose, joy, friendships, good experiences). But Scripture's vocabulary of Christian experience is rugged and stretching. Our tendency is to say 'If it hurts it cannot be truly spiritual'. But Paul's tendency is to remind us that if it is spiritual it may well hurt – someone, somewhere, sometime. No pains, no gains.

TAKING RISKS

Epaphroditus had *risked his life* in order to serve Christ by serving Paul and the Philippians (v. 30). Others had done that too (see *Rom.* 16:4). The verb Paul uses is related to the word for the money which someone in a civil law suit was required to deposit when bringing legal action against another party. It was put up as a 'stake'. If the case was lost their money was forfeited. It says a good deal about the apostle that people felt it was worth putting their lives at stake for him in this way. It says even more about the risk-taker. He counted Paul as more important than himself (cf. 2:4).

Epaphroditus teaches us that there is no such thing as a risk-free life of faith. Of course, one thing is certain – Jesus Christ. He is the same yesterday, today, and forever. It is no gamble to rest our hopes on him. Indeed, to fail to do so is to risk and lose all. When we become his, that is exactly what we are – his, and no longer our own. We have yielded control over our own lives; we count our own security in this world as subservient to our Lord's will and purposes. In that limited sense we are all risk-takers by definition.

The question is: Am I a risk-taker in fact? Have I risked anything for Christ recently?

17

Watch Out!

Finally, my brothers, rejoice in the Lord! It is no trouble for me to write the same things to you again, and it is a safeguard for you. Watch out for those dogs, those men who do evil, those mutilators of the flesh. For it is we who are the circumcision, we who worship by the Spirit of God, who glory in Christ Jesus, and who put no confidence in the flesh (Phil. 3:1–3).

The power of a great work of art often lies in the use of contrast, for example the use of light and shade in a painting, or good and evil in a novel. Paul's teaching is often like that. He underlines the wonder of grace by explaining the depths of sin; he explains the positive aspects of the Christian life by setting them in the context of the things which the Christian is to avoid.

In Philippians 2 he has shown the church how to avoid pride and disunity by pointing them to Christ's humility and to the spirit of Christ's servants Timothy and Epaphroditus. Now, in chapter three, Paul shows up false Christianity by painting a portrait of the true Christian he himself longs to be.

We are scarcely prepared for what follows, however, by the apostle's opening exhortation: *Finally . . . rejoice in the Lord* (3:1). At first glance it appears that he is actually on the point of bringing the letter to a conclusion, but is distracted by some new thoughts. In that case what he goes on to say in 4:8ff would be what was in his mind earlier, just as what Paul begins to say in Ephesians 3:1 seems to be delayed until Ephesians 4:1! Anyone who speaks in public (or listens!), or writes letters, knows how easily this happens.

'Finally', in the vocabulary of some people, does not necessarily mean the end is in sight!

It is possible that Paul did mean to draw to a conclusion here, but new information reached him and compelled him to develop a new theme; perhaps someone simply asked him as he wrote, 'Have you told them what you were talking to us about last night?' and thus stimulated Paul to develop the teaching in chapters three and four.

On the other hand, *Finally* might be better translated, 'Now, to go on . . .'. For what follows between 3:1 and 4:7 is not an incidental extra to the letter; it is part of its doctrinal and pastoral heart.

The apostle is once again concerned that the Philippians should share his joy (1:18, twice; 1:25–26; 2:18).

He now qualifies this in two ways:

(i)   He indicates that all true joy is *in the Lord* (3:1). It has its source and ultimate object in him. Paul could, of course, rejoice because of some of his circumstances, but by no means because of all of them. Our circumstances provide an all-too-fickle foundation for profound and lasting joy. But joy in the Lord is able to co-exist with all kinds of situations. Its source does not lie in our changing circumstances but in our unchanging Saviour and in the joy-giving word he has spoken to us.

This is one of the points Jesus was concerned to emphasise to his disciples before his crucifixion. He explained that their union with him was like the relationship of branches to a vine. Yes, they would experience pain and suffering; but they must see that as the Father's pruning knife preparing them to bear fruit. They must let Christ's word dwell in them, because he had spoken to them in order that his joy might be in them and their joy might be full (*John* 15:11)

(ii)   Secondly, Paul suggests that joy must be guarded if it is to be maintained.

We can sense here that Paul feels a little self-conscious about repeating teaching he has earlier given. Perhaps he was conscious of the ease with which we tend to say, 'I have heard that before; I do not need to hear it again.' Not only the ancient Athenians, but sadly some contemporary Christians, always want to hear something new and different (*Acts* 17:21). Their presence can place a subtle pressure on a teacher or preacher to produce novelty. Paul resisted that pressure; he realised the frailty of our understanding, the brevity of our memories.

Elsewhere Paul was constantly appealing to his readers 'Do you not know? Do you not remember what you were taught?' (e.g., *Rom.* 6:3, 16). We are rarely as mature as we think; we are never beyond needing the truth of Scripture explained to us again. The freshness lies not in novelty, but in the power of the Spirit helping us to see how much more wonderful and potent is the truth we already knew. Then we realise how comparatively superficial our knowledge has been.

In this connection, Paul has a specific reason for going over well-trodden ground. He believes that the Philippians may soon be confronted with destructive false teaching. He knows such teaching always destroys joy (have you noticed the joylessness there seems to be in the sects?). 'Look out!' is his message.

DOGS, EVIL-WORKERS AND MUTILATORS

There follows, in verse two, a violent warning, certainly among the strongest sentences in any of Paul's letters. He calls the unidentified seducers *dogs . . . men who do evil . . . mutilators of the flesh.* The description, however, is not simply plucked out of the apostle's street vocabulary. It is carefully chosen to reflect the fact that these teachers are actually the reverse of what they claim to be.

Most likely, the false teachers were Judaizers who insisted that in order to be a true Christian, or perhaps a 'perfect' one (contrast 3:12ff), it was necessary to add to faith in Christ faithfulness to the Old Testament ceremonial law, including circumcision.

In the eyes of the Jew, Gentiles were *dogs*, ritually unclean animals, not to be associated with, devoid of divine blessing. Paul is saying: 'These false teachers, with their Jewish teachings have so distorted the truth of the gospel that they have become like Gentile unbelievers, since they do not appreciate that our salvation is found totally in Jesus Christ.'

The false teachers evidently insisted on legal observance as a qualification for grace. But again and again Paul had taught that 'no one will be declared righteous in his [God's] sight by observing the law; rather, through the law we become conscious of sin' (*Rom.* 3:20). These teachers were not doers of good; they were overturning the only way to do good and to fulfil the law, namely exclusively through faith in Christ (see *Rom.* 3:31). They were *men who do evil*.

These teachers also insisted that circumcision was essential to salvation. But throughout his ministry Paul had taught that to add circumcision to the work of Christ was not to enhance it but to destroy it (see *Gal.* 5:2). With a striking play on words, Paul calls those who would cut off the foreskin not friends of salvation but agents of destruction; not healers but mutilators.

We perhaps find it difficult to come to terms with such strong language. Paul simply wants to make sure we have our eyes open (*Watch out . . .*) to the tragic consequences of such false teaching. It spreads like gangrene and destroys faith (*2 Tim.* 2:17–18). It is life-threatening.

TRUE GRACE

What, then, are the hallmarks of true teachers and true Christians? Paul lists them in verse three. The *true circumcision,* that is the true covenant people of God, have three characteristics:

(i) They *worship by the Spirit of God*. The old age of ritual, ceremony, and specially sanctified places has gone. To insist on that is, to Paul, like insisting on lighting a match in order to see when the sun is shining brightly!

(ii) They *glory in Christ Jesus* as their Saviour. They realise that they can do nothing to save themselves and that Christ has done everything for them. To add circumcision, or any rite to the work of Christ is, effectively, to destroy it, because it denies the sufficiency of his grace to save us.

(iii) They *put no confidence in the flesh*. Upbringing, natural qualities and gifts, possessions, traditions, an education that makes us feel superior to others – all these are irrelevant. More, when we trust in them they pull us down in sin and failure; they cannot earn us favour with God. We cannot afford to rely on them. Christ and Christ alone is our security.

This is the gospel. Dilute it, add to it, distort it – and all is lost. Believe it and we will be justified. And, being justified by such faith we will rejoice (*Rom.* 5:1, 2, 3, 11).

18

Room for Boasting?

Though I myself have reasons for such confidence. If anyone else thinks he has reasons to put confidence in the flesh, I have more: circumcised on the eighth day, of the people of Israel, of the tribe of Benjamin, a Hebrew of Hebrews; in regard to the law, a Pharisee; as for zeal, persecuting the church; as for legalistic righteousness, faultless (Phil. 3:4–6).

The Judaizers against whom Paul was warning the Philippians were not lacking in zeal; their insistence on the circumcision of adult converts, for example, underlined the level of commitment they expected from those who responded to their teaching. No doubt these false teachers pointed to certain aspects of the spirituality they taught which were apparently more demanding than first-century Christians were used to.

But zeal can be misplaced, and, equally seriously, wrongly resourced. It can be spiritually uneducated, undisciplined by the guidelines which God gives us in Scripture. And it is all too easy for young or poorly instructed Christians to be deceived by an impression of superior spirituality.

In many ways, the idea of being superior, of being able to boast in higher achievements, is the hallmark of false teaching. Paul has already indicated that. For all the apparent advanced spirituality of the false teachers, the apostle hints that their confidence was not, ultimately, in the Lord, but *in the flesh* (v. 4). It was not rooted in faith in Christ or motivated by love for him. Their zeal was 'not based on knowledge' (*Rom.* 10:2).

But how is Paul to bear effective witness over against this false teaching with its pseudo-spirituality? He was the ideal apostle to do so because of his own religious background. Can the false teachers make great claims? Paul can make greater ones: *If anyone else thinks he has reasons to put confidence in the flesh, I have more* (v. 4).

PAUL'S FORMER CONFIDENCE

These Judaizers claimed a certain religious superiority to, and practices older than, Paul's gospel. But Paul is able to point to his own background, itself superior to theirs, and argue: 'All this I have, but it profits me nothing.'

He lists seven marks in his own life that might have provided him with *reasons to put confidence in the flesh*. Four of them are inherited, three refer to his personal accomplishments.

(i)   In relation to the Jewish rite of circumcision Paul was *circumcised on the eighth day* (literally 'an eight-dayer'). The expression is used only here in the New Testament, but is one which cleverly underlines the purity of his Jewish background. He had been born in a family where the regulations of the Old Testament were kept with studied exactness. No incomer he, circumcised as a Gentile convert.

(ii)   He was *of the people of Israel* by birth (v. 5), a pure and true descendent of the great Old Testament patriarch. The privileges to which Paul refers all belonged to him as a birthright: '. . . the people of Israel. Theirs is the adoption as sons; theirs the divine glory, the covenants, the receiving of the law, the temple worship and the promises. Theirs are the patriarchs . . . ' (*Rom.* 9:4-5).

(iii)   Furthermore, Paul was *of the tribe of Benjamin,* a fact which he again mentions as significant in Romans 11:1. Benjamin was the special son of Jacob and Rachel; his birth cost his mother her life. But rather than name him 'son of my sorrow [Ben-Oni]', Jacob had called him 'son of my right hand [Benjamin]' (*Gen.* 35:18). It was from the tribe of Benjamin that Saul, Israel's first king, had emerged – a fact probably memorialised in Paul's given name.

(iv) The apostle was also *a Hebrew of Hebrews* (v. 5). He was a native Hebrew speaker brought up in a Hebrew-speaking family even although they had lived in Tarsus. So committed had his family been to Jewish orthodoxy that they sent him to study in Jerusalem under the rabbi Gamaliel who had 'thoroughly trained' him in the law (see *Acts* 22:3). It is hard to imagine a pedigree in which it would be easier to boast.

But there is more to come. These grounds for *confidence in the flesh* were inherited. Paul himself had added to his credentials by personal commitment.

(v) He had adopted the lifestyle of *a Pharisee* in relationship to the law.

The Pharisees were a Jewish sect, coming into being sometime in the second century B.C. As their name implies ('separated ones'), they were deeply committed to pure religion. In order to maintain a covenant relationship with God they strictly observed the Mosaic law. In order to accomplish this they also adhered carefully to a lengthy list of requirements which secured consistency with the law. No Judaizer of the first century could out-Judaize these men in their zeal for Old Testament religion!

(vi) Nobody among the false teachers could out-Saul Paul! Did they have zeal? Paul had formerly been so incensed by the teaching of the early Christians that he had been engaged in *persecuting the church*. He imprisoned them (*Acts* 8:3). He had even tried to force them to blaspheme (*Acts* 26:11 – no wonder he later came to regard himself as 'the worst of sinners', *1 Tim.* 1:16). He had voted for the death penalty for Christians (*Acts* 26:10), and had witnessed their execution (*Acts* 7:58, 60). Here was zeal that knew no limits to its energy.

(vii) Paul also believed himself to be, in terms of *legalistic righteousness, faultless* (v. 6). His pharisaic observance of the law was beyond reproach.

Of all these statements, this last one is often seen as the most puzzling. What does Paul mean? In particular, how can these words be reconciled with his statements in Romans 7? Is he simply describing the time when he 'was alive apart from law' (*Rom.* 7:9)? Later, he says, 'when the commandment came, sin sprang to life and I died' (*Rom.* 7:9).

Perhaps the most helpful insight into Paul's words is found in the Gospel record of the response of the young ruler to Jesus' enquiry whether he had kept the commandments. He believed he had done so from boyhood (*Mark* 10:17–25). The fact that 'Jesus looked at him and loved him' (*Mark* 10:21) suggests that this response was not the fabrication of a hypocrite. But it was the reaction of someone who sees the law only as a series of external regulations.

Such law-keeping is a phenomenal achievement. Jesus did not despise it. But it misses the main point, as his challenge to sell everything and follow him makes plain. It gives the impression that we are right with God. But the law was given, in part, to reveal our sinfulness, to reveal (as Jesus' challenge to the ruler demonstrated) that we have dethroned God from the centre of our lives and there raised an altar where self is worshipped.

Saul of Tarsus had made a similar tragic mistake. It is significant to reflect on the event that stopped him in his tracks and began to bring him to realise his spiritual bankruptcy. Indeed, that providential incident may be the reason he responds to these zealous false teachers by means of a personal testimony.

Saul had seen a Christian, a contemporary whose righteousness surpassed his own (*Matt.* 5:20), whose love for the faith of the Old Testament and whose appreciation of the prophets pointed him towards Christ rather than against him – a young man prepared to die for his risen Lord. In dying he had displayed the grace, the forgiveness, the certainty of salvation to which the Old Testament bore eloquent witness. Stephen, the martyr had experienced what all the zeal and law-keeping of Saul of Tarsus could not bring. Stephen had Christ, and having Christ meant everything (*Acts* 7:55–60). Saul had only the bare bones of Pharisaic rule-keeping; without Christ he had nothing.

Every reason we have for *confidence in the flesh*, be it family background or religious upbringing and activity, withers before Paul's testimony. He is simply telling us all that it is possible to be and to have, and yet not be a true believer and not have salvation because in all our having we do not yet have Christ.

Think about it. Make sure the root of the matter is in you.

19

Christ is Gain

*But whatever was to my profit I now consider loss for the sake of
Christ. What is more, I consider everything a loss compared to
the surpassing greatness of knowing Christ Jesus my Lord, for
whose sake I have lost all things. I consider them rubbish, that I
may gain Christ and be found in him, not having a righteousness
of my own that comes from the law, but that which is through
faith in Christ – the righteousness that comes from God and is by
faith. I want to know Christ and the power of his resurrection
and the fellowship of sharing in his sufferings, becoming like him
in his death, and so, somehow, to attain to the resurrection from
the dead* (Phil. 3:7–11).

Paul had turned his back on self-confidence of every kind when
he became a Christian. But to what did he turn? Better still, to
whom did he turn? He answers the question in the verses which
follow. They are among the most revealing words the apostle has
given us. They express the central ambition of his life. They also
take us to the very heart of the gospel. The more clearly we understand what he is saying the easier it is to appreciate why he no
longer placed his confidence in the flesh.

LOSS

In Philippians 3:4–6, Paul had mentioned the many advantages
that were his by birth and attainment. But now he calculates their
true worth in the light of the gospel. What is the *profit* they provide
in relation to salvation?

We should not think the question is naive. At one time even the church spoke of a treasury of merits to which the extra righteousness of the saints could be contributed (their supererogatory merit, to give it the technical term). It was assumed that an individual could not only be acceptable to God, but in a sense more than acceptable.

Paul sees through such muddled thinking with great penetration. It is a grave miscalculation; the truth is that everything Paul might have counted as 'profit' was actually 'loss' (v. 7). Lest we fail to grasp his point he repeats it in three different ways in verse eight: everything is a *loss* compared to Christ; in order to know Christ he has *lost all things;* he now considers them *rubbish.*

This vivid accounting language reminds us that the message of the gospel of Christ is a tremendous shock to the system. By nature we tend to assume ourselves to be as good as the next man, and therefore just as acceptable to God as most others are. Our false thinking leads us to conclude that what we are and have achieved ought to gain us entrance into heaven. The terrible truth, however, is that it disqualifies us from heaven. What we count as profit with God is actually loss.

Think of someone going over their cheque book. All month long they have been passing pieces of paper through the banking system; they have made a note of the total amount. Then the bank statement arrives; they discover to their horror that instead of money going into their account it has been going out of it; each cheque deposited was debited, not credited. Instead of being in profit they are in loss. Not only is the situation serious, it is the very reverse of what they thought it was. It is not even as though they are in a neutral position; they are in deep debt.

So it was for Paul. His whole view of himself was turned on its head. Instead of being accepted with God, he discovered he was rejected; instead of having gone further in holiness than Christians like Stephen, he had completely lost the way; the very things he was counting on to gain righteousness with God turned out to be witnesses for the prosecution against him. All he counted on as his accomplishments were in fact his failures!

No wonder he says, *whatever was to my profit I now consider loss.* He well expresses the vigour of his discovery when he calls his previous achievements *rubbish* (v. 8). The word actually means 'excrement' and is appropriately translated in the Authorized (King James) Version as 'dung'. Compared to Christ, all is garbage.

We are very near to the secret of Paul's Christian life here. There is a direct connection between the extent to which he felt this shock and the usefulness of his life in serving God. He was overwhelmed with a sense of the utter futility of life without Christ. He saw that he had been building castles in the air. Now that they had collapsed he lived with a heart that felt keenly the unrecognised predicament of those around him who continued to make the mistake from which he had been graciously delivered.

But if this was the loss Paul suffered, he knew that he had gained much now that he belonged to Christ.

CHRIST IS GAIN

Paul had yielded up everything for Christ. No knowledge could now compare with the knowledge of Jesus (vv. 7–8). This meant fellowship with Christ, or union with him, in which all that Christ had done for him in his life, death, resurrection and ascension was brought into his life through the ministry of the Holy Spirit. This implied three things:

(i) Full justification. Paul was now *found in Christ*. He no longer approached God on the basis of his own achievements, but covered in the *righteousness* of his risen Saviour. Christ had been made sin for him; now he had been declared righteous with *the righteousness that comes from God* (v. 9; cf. *2 Cor.* 5:21). In a sense Paul was now viewed by God as being as righteous as Jesus, because he was righteous with Jesus' righteousness – *the righteousness that comes . . . by faith* (v. 9).

It is vital to grasp the implication of such justification. It is God's declaration about us; it depends on what Christ has done, not on our works. Furthermore, it is complete and final. We cannot add to or subtract from it any more than we can reverse Christ's resurrection (in which God declared him righteous and demonstrated that his sacrifice had been accepted, *Rom.* 4:25). Justification is full because it gives us Christ's righteousness; it is final because it does not depend on our keeping *the law* but on God's gift of his Son; it cannot be reversed; it can never be destroyed. It is invincible, because it is the judgment of the last day brought into the present day.

(ii) Ongoing sanctification. Paul knows Christ. But he wants *to know Christ* more and more. He wants his fellowship with him to be sweeter and deeper.

This means that our union with Christ develops into a living communion with him in his *death* and *resurrection*. Notice the striking order of the statements in verse ten. Paul wants *to know Christ* in *the power of his resurrection and the fellowship of sharing in his sufferings, becoming like him in his death.* We would normally expect the opposite order (death first, then resurrection). But Paul leads us to a central element in Christian experience: it is as we live in Christ our risen Saviour that he leads us on to *the fellowship of sharing in his sufferings.*

To the Colossians Paul says 'I fill up in my flesh what is still lacking in regard to Christ's afflictions, for the sake of his body, which is the church' (*Col.* 1:24). He does not mean that he shares in Christ's atoning work, but that as God uses him and conforms him to Christ, he employs sufferings to do so.

Paul knew that this work was not yet finished. So here, he confesses that he wants to know more about this mysterious, life-transforming working of God.

(iii) Anticipated glorification. The end result of such fellowship with Christ is that *somehow* Paul will *attain to the resurrection* and experience salvation in its full and final form.

Somehow does not denote Paul's doubt whether Christ can do this but his amazement that he will do it in one like himself, full of imperfection and weakness. Will it be so? How can it be so, when he was formerly such a sinner and even now has not attained perfection (3:12)?

Here, in a nutshell, lies the difference between Saul of Tarsus and Paul the apostle. For the unconverted Saul nothing would have surprised him less than hearing that he would be saved and among the people of God on the day of resurrection. After all, he had every reason to have confidence.

But then came 'The Damascus Road Crash'! His gain became loss, his confidence boosters lay in shreds around him. Now he knew that in and of himself he was utterly unworthy of God, of heaven, of salvation. But Christ had sought him, humbled him, saved him. No wonder all he wanted now was to know Christ!

Is that what you want most of all, too?

20

Called to Perfection

Not that I have already obtained all this, or have already been made perfect, but I press on to take hold of that for which Christ Jesus took hold of me. Brothers, I do not consider myself yet to have taken hold of it. But one thing I do: Forgetting what is behind and straining towards what is ahead, I press on towards the goal to win the prize for which God has called me heavenwards in Christ Jesus. All of us who are mature should take such a view of things. And if on some point you think differently, that too God will make clear to you. Only let us live up to what we have already attained (Phil. 3:12–16).

Jesus Christ meant everything to Paul. He had made that clear: 'to me, to live is Christ and to die is gain' (1:21). Now, in chapter three, he has explained in detail what that meant: knowing Christ as the risen Lord empowering him; sharing in the fellowship of his sufferings as he was progressively conformed to him; anticipating the consummation of this fellowship in the resurrection.

Clearly the apostle was a 'goal-setter'. In various places in his letters he indicates that he had clearly defined hopes and plans. These goals seem to fit into three related categories. Some of them were short-term goals for building up the church or advancing the apostolic mission; others were long-term ambitions for his development as an apostle; some were commitments to life-long progress as a Christian. Romans 15:17–29 gives an illustration of the first kind; Colossians 1:24–29 of the second kind; Philippians 3:10–11 is a powerful illustration of the third kind.

Christians throughout the ages have imitated this wise practice. Ordering one's life has become the theme of many books and seminars, both Christian and secular. It is interesting, however, to note two features of the goal-setting described here.

(i)   Paul's goal-setting was centred on the person of Jesus Christ; it involved the pursuit of personal knowledge of Christ. Fellowship with him was his passion. Anything less can hardly be described as *Christian* goal-setting or life-management. In being stimulated by the contemporary recovery of the idea of life and time management and goal-setting Christians must not allow themselves to be deceived into thinking that the accomplishment of *impersonal* goals, objectively measurable achievements, is the same thing as true spiritual growth.

(ii)   Paul engaged in a measure of healthy self-examination. He realised that, given the nature of his great goal, there would always be a sense in which he fell short. It is an in-built factor in the nature of Christian goals that seeking to fulfil them can never bring us to the point of self-satisfaction.

AN IMPORTANT CONFESSION

It is significant that Paul confesses that he was not yet *perfect* (v. 12). In doing so he may well be contrasting himself as a true disciple with the claims of the false teachers he feared might influence the Philippians with their talk of 'perfection'. It was important for him to do this for two reasons:

(i)   So elevated is his ambition of knowing Christ, that weaker Christians might begin to doubt whether they really were genuine Christians because they knew so little of this glorious knowledge. As a true pastor, Paul is concerned to identify himself with his fellow-Christians; he is still on the road, with much ground to cover; he is a fellow-pilgrim.

(ii)   So strong and apparently spiritual is the claim to have experienced perfection that less-well-instructed Christians can easily be deceived by it. In fact, it seems to answer a deep longing every Christian knows: we long to be free from sin and failure! Conscious of the affection and respect the Philippian Christians had for him, Paul uses his own testimony to help them think clearly. If, after such wide spiritual experience and usefulness, displaying such Christ-centred zeal, Paul is not yet perfect (v. 12), then the Philippians should be wary of those who claim to be – especially when their lifestyles indicate how far short they fall of the fellowship of Christ's sufferings (see vv. 18–19).

THE PATH TO PERFECTION

Three stages to the full and final knowledge of Christ are traced in verses twelve to fourteen.

(i)   God calls us to it. God had called Paul *heavenwards in Christ Jesus* (v. 14). That call was like the starter's pistol sounding in the ears of an athlete; the race for *the prize* was on. By *calling* (e.g., *Rom.* 8:30; *Gal.* 1:6, 15; *1 Thess.* 2:12; *2 Tim.* 1:9) Paul means a summons which produces its desired effect.

We do not know exactly when this call began to register in Paul's heart. Perhaps he caught a syllable or two of it as he watched Stephen die. He was soon overwhelmed by it on the road to Damascus. We do not hear the voice of Christ in the same audible fashion; but the call which the Spirit brings to our hearts through the word of God is no less real and powerful. It is no less heavenly either – in both its origin and its destiny.

Every Christian has been called *heavenwards in Christ Jesus.* Just as men and women are called-up for military duty in times of war, this call comes with an absolute authority. But think what it means. The great God is here summoning us to enter his presence through the work of his Son. He wants us in heaven with him!

(ii)   Christ holds us to it. We have been *called* by God in Christ *to win the prize.* But the Christian life is not a brief sprint; it is a marathon race over a life-long course. In it there is much difficult terrain to be covered. We will often be like the novice pilgrim of Psalm 121 who lifted his eyes to the road that wound its way through the dangerous hills towards Jerusalem and asked, 'Where will my help come from?' 'From the Lord' was the answer then (*Psa.* 121:1–2); it is always the answer.

Paul knew that Christ *took hold* of him on the Damascus road. That hold is the reason for our spiritual security too. We will persevere to the end of the race because he keeps us going.

This is simply the teaching of Jesus. Those who are called are kept: 'My sheep listen to my voice . . . I give them eternal life, and they shall never perish; no one can snatch them out of my hand' (*John* 10:27–28; see also *1 Pet.* 1:3–5).

(iii) Paul pressed on to it. Rather than look back to see how far he had travelled in his pilgrimage, Paul pressed on towards Christ (v. 12). He resisted an all-too-subtle temptation that comes to Christians in the mid-years of their spiritual journey: to feel that they have come a reasonable distance. Why is that a mistake? Because we cannot look back and simultaneously keep our eyes fixed on Christ! So Paul repeats himself: he forgets *what is behind* and strains forwards (v. 13); he presses on *towards the goal* (v. 14). He is flat out for Christ.

NOT SINLESS, BUT MATURE

We do not reach perfection in this life (although we will when Christ returns, v. 21). Yet we do not remain in spiritual infancy and immaturity throughout our lives. In fact one of the signs of maturity will be the developing ability to forget what has passed. In natural life those who are always thinking and talking about the past rarely appreciate that. To live in the past is to hide from the reality of the present and the challenges of the future. Those who are mature in Christ will be characterised by a whole-hearted pursuit of fellowship with him which looks to the future.

A desire for Christ is the unifying hallmark of those who have begun to grow spiritually. Yes, Paul acknowledges that in various other areas we do not yet see things in the same way. But, he assures us, if the Lord has brought us to a common mind about Jesus Christ he will progressively bring us to a common mind about secondary things too.

Would such an acknowledgement of imperfection and differences among the Philippians not lead to them settling for second best? Not so long as Paul is their teacher! They may not have arrived yet at a perfect understanding of the gospel or perfect knowledge of Christ; but that is no excuse for failing to live consistently with the wonderful knowledge they do already have (v. 16). They have been called to receive *the prize* of full and unclouded knowledge of Christ and fellowship with him. Already they know him. How could they ease up now?

21

To Imitate or to Avoid

Join with others in following my example, brothers, and take note of those who live according to the pattern we gave you. For, as I have often told you before and now say again even with tears, many live as enemies of the cross of Christ. Their destiny is destruction, their god is their stomach, and their glory is in their shame. Their mind is on earthly things (Phil. 3:17–19).

To know Christ is the Christian's ambition. In the previous verses Paul has elaborated on the meaning and implications of this. In the course of doing so he had used his own experience by way of illustration. He pressed on towards the goal; he had not yet arrived at it. Now he explicitly urges the Philippians to look on and follow him as an example.

IMITATION

'Imitate me' says Paul, 'and imitate those whose lives reflect the model we set before you in our preaching and teaching' (v. 17). Strange words indeed for someone who, in his previous breath, has told us that he is not perfect! Is he now blinded by his own self-conceit, talking as though he had arrived spiritually? After all, we usually say to others, 'Do not imitate me; imitate Christ.'

The fact that Paul appeals to his readers as *brothers* in verse seventeen indicates that he had not lost his sense of proportion. Of course Christians are brothers, but in fact Paul tends to use this term of affection only at points of increased emotion, and particularly when he is expressing his deep pastoral concern.

There is no spiritual megalomania here. Paul has a realistic recognition of the nature of salvation and the way in which Christ has constituted his people. Salvation means being transformed into Christ's likeness (*Rom.* 8:29; *2 Cor.* 3:18). God's people are therefore living illustrations (albeit imperfect ones) of Jesus himself. God works in us by his Spirit to produce the graces which were so evident in Jesus himself. He makes his people display fragments of Christ's image, reflections of his glory. In them the *pattern* (v. 17) of Christ's own life is reproduced.

Paul realised that he could not appeal to the Philippians to follow his teaching if they were not able to see it lived out in flesh-and-blood terms in his own life as an *example*.

It is generally true that until we see what the teaching of the gospel looks like in someone's life we do not really understand what it means. That is why the preaching of the gospel can never be isolated from the life of the church. Only when non-Christians see the power of the gospel in people they know are they likely to respond to it.

Paul may have learned the lesson of the importance of Christians being models of the gospel in the events which surrounded his own conversion. In his death Stephen had wonderfully reflected the grace of his Lord Jesus; his dying words of forgiveness were an echo of the words which his Saviour had uttered from the cross. Saul of Tarsus must have found his Christ-likeness unnerving (*Acts* 7:54–60).

There was another reason why this principle was so important for the Philippians: they did not have the entire New Testament as we do. They may have had more parts of it than this one letter (see *Col.* 4:16 for an example of the way in which apostolic letters came into the possession of more than one church). But they did not even have the total teaching of Paul. Think of living the Christian life without Romans! For that reason the role of the apostle's example was tremendously important. Answering the questions, 'What did Paul do? How did Paul think, in a situation like this?' gave the first Christians guidance until the day came when the entire New Testament was available to them.

At the root of Paul's exhortation is the principle he states clearly in 1 Corinthians 11:1: 'Follow my example, as I follow the example of Christ.' They could follow Paul *because* he followed Christ: we should follow fellow-Christians only insofar as they follow Christ.

Do we look for, admire, and imitate the Christ-likeness we see in others? Do we pray for ourselves lest we cause others to stumble by bringing shame to the name of our Lord? Do we pray that others will catch a glimpse of Christ through what we are and want to trust, know and love him better?

This is a responsibility we cannot avoid. It is written into the principles of the kingdom of God.

AVOIDANCE

There is one final reason why Paul appeals to his brethren in Philippi to follow his example: they will be exposed to other teachers. Their integrity can be tested by the example they set (*Matt.* 7:15–20).

Paul was too wise a pastor to assume that everyone who professed to be a teacher of the faith was faithful to Christ. He was also too sensitive a Christian to speak about this without deep feeling: there were *tears* on his cheeks as he wrote (v. 18).

We cannot be absolutely certain about the identity of those against whom Paul warns his brothers here. Because of their claims to perfection, some scholars believe they must be a different group from the Judaizers Paul had opposed earlier in the chapter. But it is quite possible that an emphasis on Old Testament regulations co-existed with a claim to perfection. Sadly, the history of the church – including its recent history – suggests that teachers who lay down the strictest (and most legalistic) standards for their disciples may themselves be slaves of their own lusts, as Paul indicates here.

Whatever the specific identity of these people, the great value in what Paul says about them lies in the three tests he gives us for discerning false teachers and their teaching.

(i)   They *live as enemies of the cross of Christ* (v. 18). The cross is the touchstone of both true doctrine and true practice. When we hear new teaching, or when a preacher or teacher is given special prominence, we must always ask: 'What does he say (or *not* say) about the cross?' 'What place does the cross have in their lives?' Can they say with Paul, 'May I never boast except in the cross of our Lord Jesus Christ, through which the world has been crucified to me, and I to the world' (*Gal.* 6:14)? That is the test. Where the cross (Christ's death as the means of the forgiveness of sins) is denied or ignored, there we may begin to suspect enemies of the cross of Christ, however plausible they may at first seem.

(ii) *Their god is their stomach* (v. 19). The word translated here *stomach* probably has a broader meaning such as 'sensual appetites'. Not only is the doctrine of the cross denied in the preaching of these teachers, its significance for Christian living is repudiated in their lives. Do they teach and live out a lifestyle which involves following Christ in self-denying devotion to God and love for others? Or, are their lives marked by a sad self-indulgence?

(iii) *Their mind is on earthly things* (v. 19). In Paul's days there were preachers and teachers whose ambition was to acquire wealth for themselves rather than to store up treasure in heaven. They were attracted by possessions, reputation and position. These were the things that filled their minds and the hidden agenda behind all of their activities (cf. *2 Cor.* 4:2). There is a cast of mind that betrays the message of the gospel. Look out for it.

The *destiny* of such false teachers is *destruction* (v. 19). That is inevitable when they *glory* in what is really *shame* (v. 19).

The message is clear. Follow Christ, the crucified Saviour, and those whose lives provide Christ-like examples. Do not set your mind *on earthly things* like them, and be on your guard against their teaching and influence. Christ is the goal; Christ and him crucified is the message; taking up the cross is the way he calls us to live. Follow him; follow Paul as he boasts only of Christ and his cross; follow those who walk that narrow way. It may be that there are others who are watching and will follow you.

22

Citizens of Heaven

But our citizenship is in heaven. And we eagerly await a Saviour from there, the Lord Jesus Christ, who, by the power that enables him to bring everything under his control, will transform our lowly bodies so that they will be like his glorious body. Therefore, my brothers, you whom I love and long for, my joy and crown, that is how you should stand firm in the Lord, dear friends! (Phil. 3:20–4:1).

Paul has been emphasising the significance of examples and models in the Christian life: some are to be imitated; others need to be avoided. In particular he draws our attention to the characteristics which often manifest themselves in the lives of those who are false teachers.

The apostle's writings all give expression to an underlying principle (to which he returns on several occasions in this letter): how we think influences how we live. That is as true of false teaching as it is of Christian truth. And so Paul tries to indicate to his readers that those who teach false doctrine will, eventually, express the falsehood of their doctrine by moral deviation in their lives. In Philippians 3:18-19 he had pointed out four such features in the lives of the false teachers:

(i)   In character they were enemies of the cross of Christ.

(ii) Their god was their own passions.

(iii) Their glory was in the shame in which they indulged.

(iv) Their future was destruction.

In what follows, he shows us that at each of these points the lives of Christians stand in contrast in terms of their character, their Lord, their glory, and their destiny.

CHRISTIAN CHARACTER

Their *citizenship is in heaven* (v. 20). Christians are aliens or strangers in this world (*1 Pet.* 1:1; 2:11). Their true home is in Christ, in the presence of God.

Paul gives that idea a fine touch here, however. We have already noted that Philippi had become a Roman colony during the previous century. It was governed by Roman law; its inhabitants wore Roman dress; they used Latin in official documents; even the architecture of Philippi became Romanesque in character. Most significantly of all, the citizens of Philippi had the privilege of being citizens of Rome.

To live in Philippi, but to be a citizen of Rome, living the Roman life while absent from the Roman capital – what an ideal illustration of the Christian! We are in Christ; we have experienced a heavenly calling; we belong to another country and are citizens of a different city from this world. Our character is bound to be different. We inevitably stand out for our mind is not on earthly things. In fact we *eagerly await* Someone who is coming from heaven (vv. 19–20).

THE LORD FROM HEAVEN

'Their god is their stomach' Paul had said of the false teachers (v. 19); they worshipped downwards and inwards! They needed to feed their god in order to keep him alive! But contrast the Christian believer who looks upward, outward and forward to his Lord and God, *the Lord Jesus Christ* (v. 20; cf. *Tit.* 2:13).

What future is there in the object of your devotion? is a question which should never be far from our minds. What future does the god passion hold out to us? No doubt, as the author of Hebrews says, sin does bring its pleasures (*Heb.* 11:25); but they are 'for a short time'. By contrast only 'Jesus Christ is the same yesterday and today and forever' (*Heb.* 13:8).

There is a future with him, as well as a present. Those whose 'mind is on earthly things' (v. 19) live only for the present, to gratify their desires. They know neither satisfaction in this life nor the hope of true joy in the world to come. Christians, by contrast, have the blessings of grace now and eagerly look forward then to their Saviour coming from heaven to take them where they belong.

How different the spirit of the Christian is from those who are dominated by the spirit of this world!

THE CHRISTIAN'S GLORY

The false teachers' 'glory is in their shame' (v. 19). By contrast Christians look forward to all that is shameful giving way to glory.

Jesus Christ will come from heaven as our *Saviour* (v. 20). But he will also come as the *Lord* who will exercise his authority over the whole creation. He has *power that enables him to bring everything under his control* (v. 21). One day he will display it universally.

Think of the drama of the occasion, as Paul himself did regularly:

> Just as we have borne the likeness of the
>   earthly man, so shall we bear the likeness
>   of the man from heaven . . .
> We will all be changed – in a flash, in the
>   twinkling of an eye, at the last trumpet.
> For the trumpet will sound,
>   the dead will be raised imperishable,
>   and we will be changed.
>   (*1 Cor.* 15:49, 51–52)

We have a future to which not all the immediate gratification in the world can compare! We will be like Christ, for he *will transform our lowly bodies so that they will be like his glorious body* (v. 21). Then our salvation will be complete.

From beginning to end salvation is a process of transforming us into the likeness of Christ. At first that involves being given heavenly birth into his family (see *John* 3); throughout our lives the graces of Christ are increasingly reproduced in us. Now Paul comes to the staggering finale: these *lowly bodies,* made from the dust of the earth (*Gen.* 2:7), weakened by sin and disease, subject to the shame of death and disintegration, will be transformed by Christ when he raises them from the dust. 'The body that is sown is perishable, it is raised imperishable; it is sown in dishonour, it is raised in glory; it is sown in weakness, it is raised in power; it is sown a natural body, it is raised a spiritual body [not an 'insubstantial' body, but a body suited to life in the power of the Spirit]' (*1 Cor.* 15:42–44). What glory!

TO CROWN IT ALL

The Christian's future is not merely a topic of idle speculation for the New Testament writers; it is always a spur to action and a cause of joy (see, for example, *2 Pet.* 3:11; *1 John* 3:1–3). Paul now sets his own life in the context of the return of his Master. As he looks to the future he thinks about the enduring significance of his relationship to the Philippians. In language similar to 1 Thessalonians 2:19–20 he calls them his *joy and crown* (4:1).

The Philippians were his brothers; he loved them and longed for them. Unlike the shameful things to which the false teachers devoted themselves, this relationship would last. More than that, it too would be transformed into something glorious – into Paul's *joy and crown*. Heaven, and the Philippians too, would be his.

Live for the things that will last! That is the underlying lesson. Paul has shown us what this means: living for the long-term, and not with an eye on the quick and easy methods of spiritual advance which are so characteristic of false teachers. That means keeping our eye fixed on eternal realities, on the long-term harvest of our lives, not on short term satisfaction. It means lifting our eyes to the sure promise that Christ will appear again in glory, rather than lowering our eyes to ourselves and our appetites. The only enduring appetite is an appetite of love for Christ and his people. All else will become dust.

No wonder when faced with the choice between Christ and this world Paul always chose Christ. As a result he was able to live joyfully even in this world.

Is that the kind of example I follow?

23

Agreeing and Helping

*I plead with Euodia and I plead with Syntyche to agree with
each other in the Lord. Yes, and I ask you, loyal yoke-fellow,
help these women who have contended at my side in the cause
of the gospel, along with Clement and the rest of my fellow-
workers whose names are in the book of life* (Phil. 4:2–3).

At first sight the closing chapter of Paul's Letter to the Philippians
seems to be a series of haphazard comments and counsel.
This should not really surprise us. Paul himself did not divide his
writings into chapters and verses; he wrote *letters*. As those who
still write and receive personal letters know, there is a tendency
towards the end of a letter to write brief pieces of news, short
greetings, and (of course!) to add things that were forgotten earlier.

But a closer examination of Philippians 4 suggests that there is
more to this chapter than meets the eye. Like other closing sections
in Paul's letters it actually suggests various illustrations and
applications of the teaching contained in the body of the letter.

CHRISTIAN ATTITUDES

The various themes briefly treated throughout the chapter can be
summarised under the general topic of Christian attitudes.

The verb 'to think' (variously translated) occurs with some
frequency in Philippians (1:7; 2:2 [twice]; 2:5; 3:15; 3:19; 4:2; 4:10
[twice]). As we have seen, Paul was convinced that what we think,
and the way we think, profoundly influences the way we live.

Fundamental to his exposition of this principle was the teaching in chapter two in which he had stressed that those who are united to Christ should share the attitude of Christ. Here that principle is further applied. In verse two the same verb is translated *agree with;* in verse ten it is translated by the idea of concern. The conviction that thinking influences living reappears under the guise of a different verb in verse eight: 'think about such things'. Here, in verses two and three, he concentrates on the way Christians should think in the context of their Christian fellowship.

AGREEING TOGETHER

The Philippians meant everything to Paul; they were his 'joy and crown' (v. 1). He wanted them to mean everything to each other.

There had been a breakdown in that kind of fellowship at Philippi. It was associated with two of the women in the congregation, *Euodia and . . . Syntyche.* The details are, tactfully, not discussed by Paul. But the situation was obviously serious enough for him to address these women by name, and the division sufficiently long-standing for news of it to have reached Paul's ears.

The situation here is very different from Paul's concern over the threat of false teachers. They were 'enemies of the cross' (3:18); but these women had been (and Paul still regarded them as) *fellow-workers* who had struggled with the apostle *in the cause of the gospel.* Unlike those whose 'destiny is destruction' (3:19) Paul could include these ladies *with Clement* and others *whose names are in the book of life* (v. 3). He was sure they were genuine believers. Nevertheless there was a division between them.

This division was, no doubt, affecting the entire church. Paul's first preaching in Macedonia was at a prayer-gathering beside the river where the missionaries 'began to speak to the women who had gathered there' (*Acts* 16:13). The apostolic band had been offered hospitality by Lydia, and it may well be that a congregation later met in her house. If Euodia and Syntyche were among that original little group of praying women, a disagreement between them had potentially far-reaching repercussions.

This incidental section thus has a significance far beyond the two women whose names are mentioned. Disagreements between influential, or founding members of a fellowship can be very serious indeed. The apostolic appeal to agree needs to be heeded. But how? Paul mentions three things which provide direction.

THE RECIPE FOR HARMONY

(i)   Firstly, Christians are to learn *to agree* (literally, 'to think the same things') *in the Lord*.

How can two people who think differently be brought to think in the same way? By remembering that they are both 'in the Lord'. They are his, not their own; they are both his. It would be inconsistent, therefore, for either of them to insist on her own way, when they both belonged to a Saviour who had not insisted on his way nor sought to please himself (cf. 2:1–11; *Rom.* 15:2–3). Their Lord made himself nothing, did not grasp at his rights. He took the role of a servant (2:6–7). In the Lord they were called to follow his example in their relationships with each other.

We can never shake hands with a fellow-Christian after a disagreement and say 'I told you so.' Instead we must always say, 'The Lord has told both of us so.'

(ii)   Secondly, Christians have been given insight into the mind of the Lord. He had shown the Philippians his will and purposes not only in the incarnation, but in the revelation he had provided in apostolic teaching and example. Paul's life had set before them an 'example' (3:17); his teaching had given them the 'pattern' (3:17) for living.

The contemporary application of this is obvious. When two Christians disagree, they must both seek to submit their thinking to the teaching of Scripture. That is the litmus test of our real attitude. This challenge will immediately reveal a disagreement that is due to self-centredness or pride. Do we insist that our way is the right way, irrespective of what the Lord's way is? Sadly that is often the case. If, as we have seen, the secret of unity is humility, its corollary is that the chief cause of division is pride.

(iii) Thirdly, Paul makes clear that division between two individuals in a Christian fellowship can never remain a private matter between them. It inevitably affects others. Sometimes, sadly, it means that we insist that those we know must take our side of the disagreement if they are to remain in fellowship with us. That was the attitude of the invidious Diotrephes (*2 John* vv. 9–10). It is a recipe for poisoning the entire church.

Because disagreements do not remain private, Paul appeals not only to the individuals involved but to at least one other person to help them. *Loyal yoke-fellow* (v. 3) is the NIV text's translation of the more literal *loyal* [or, perhaps, 'aptly named'] *Syzygus* (see NIV footnote). It is possible that Paul has an individual, named Syzygus, in mind, although this does not seem to occur elsewhere as a first century name. Various suggestions have been made to identify this person. These include Epaphroditus (addressed in the letter on the assumption that he would be present when it was read to the whole church), and even Paul's wife (someone otherwise non-existent in the New Testament!).

Christian fellowships are often at their worst when dealing with differences of opinion. In some ways biblically-based churches find it easier to deal with false teaching. But personal differences can be almost as deadly, dividing the fellowship, sowing seeds of bitterness, diverting attention from central issues to sometimes petty, peripheral concerns, sucking energy that should be employed in building up believers and in reaching out to the community. How effectively we handle these differences may say more about the biblical character of our church life than how we handle heresy.

There is a sting in the tail here. What must Paul's yoke-fellow have felt when he or she was singled out to help in this situation? How do you respond when the Spirit lays his hand on you as the person responsible to help heal division?

Paul here gives us the guidelines to use.

24

Vital Relationships

*Rejoice in the Lord always. I will say it again: Rejoice! Let
your gentleness be evident to all. The Lord is near. Do not be
anxious about anything, but in everything, by prayer and
petition, with thanksgiving, present your requests to God.
And the peace of God, which transcends all understanding,
will guard your hearts and your minds in Christ Jesus.
Finally, brothers, whatever is true, whatever is noble, whatever is right, whatever is pure, whatever is lovely, whatever is
admirable – if anything is excellent or praiseworthy – think
about such things. Whatever you have learned or received or
heard from me, or seen in me – put it into practice. And the
God of peace will be with you* (Phil. 4:4–9).

Much that Paul writes in the closing exhortations of Philippians
focuses on the way in which Christians think, and the themes
which are to occupy our minds. Verses two and three stressed the
importance of submitting our minds to the revelation God has
given us in apostolic teaching; this is certainly the remedy for
potential divisions in a Christian fellowship. Now the apostle turns
our attention to the mindset which should govern our ordinary
daily experience.

This involves our relationship to Christ, to others, and to
ourselves.

RELATIONSHIP TO CHRIST

We are to *rejoice in the Lord always* (v. 4). Lest we fail to hear him,
or hearing him are incapable of taking in what he is saying, Paul
repeats himself: *I will say it again: Rejoice!*

An emphasis on joy runs through Philippians, as we have seen. But two things are distinctive about these words. First, Paul speaks about an ongoing and permanently renewed joy. It is to be theirs *always*. Second, Paul exhorts, indeed commands them to *rejoice*.

This may strike us as unusual, if not impossible, because we have sometimes been misled into thinking of joy, just as we tend to think of love, as primarily a matter of feelings and spontaneous emotions. These, by definition, cannot be commanded; they simply happen. But that is a distortion of the biblical teaching.

God made men and women capable of thinking, willing and feeling. In the divine design, our thinking was meant to be informed, shaped and governed by his revelation. We were created to think God's thoughts after him, as it is sometimes put. Such thought processes inevitably inform, influence and direct our powers of volition. We understand what is right and good, and we commit our wills to accomplishing it. In turn our feelings are moulded by what we think and will. In a rightly-ordered life, emotions or feelings are directed to what is good and gracious; these things are desired and loved. Our feelings and emotions are not isolated from our thinking and willing but guided by them.

That order was overturned by sin; it always is. Our wills now tend to be dominated by our feelings; our thoughts are often ruled by our wills. Because of sin we are able to rejoice only when we feel good. By contrast Paul is telling us to rejoice no matter what we feel.

How is that possible? His words, *Rejoice in the Lord* provide the answer. This joy is not based on how we feel about our personal circumstances, but on the fact of our fellowship with Christ, and on the facts about him. 'Think about that,' Paul is saying, 'and you will be able to taste joy whatever the circumstances.'

The recipe for joy is given to us by Jesus himself. Immediately before his betrayal he spoke to the disciples, assuring them that they would experience it despite the grief that was about to come upon them. Explaining to them the closeness of their union with him, he says: 'I have told you this that my joy may be in you and that your joy may be complete' (*John* 15:11). When his words 'dwell' in them (*John* 15:7), influencing the way they think more powerfully than do their circumstances, then they will rejoice.

Thus, says Paul, those who have grasped the biblical truth that they are justified by grace through faith in Christ are able to rejoice even in their sufferings (*Rom.* 5:1–3). Here is a joy that transcends immediate circumstances.

RELATIONSHIPS TO OTHERS

Our *gentleness* is to be *extended to all* (v. 5), in the way we are patient and kindly in our dealings with others.

This command seems unrelated to the exhortation to *rejoice;* but there is a connection. The people who are joyful are those who have been delivered from an obsession with themselves and their immediate circumstances. But that is also a prerequisite to being *gentle.* The joyless person can never be a gentle person.

Paul gives us a specific reason for this quality: *The Lord is near* (v. 5). But in what sense? Most students of this passage understand Paul's words as a reference to Christ's return. His coming is near at hand.

The teaching of the New Testament is that Christ's death, resurrection, and ascension ushered in the dawn of 'the last days'. Since the coming of the Holy Spirit at Pentecost, there is only one great event to come to complete God's work of salvation: the return of Christ.

From this perspective, the return of Christ is always *near.* Consequently Paul believed that Christians must always be ready for that great day. He himself seems to have been open to the possibility that it might take place during his own lifetime, although he was also aware that it might not. (His teaching in 1 Thessalonians 4:13–18 covers both possibilities.)

Paul is then saying: Live daily with the expectation that the Lord will return as your Saviour, and also as the Judge of the world. Let that thought create a spirit of gentleness in you. For you know him as Saviour; he has been gentle with you although you deserve his judgment.

But Christ is near in another sense: 'The Lord is close to the brokenhearted and saves those who are crushed in spirit' (*Psa.* 34:18).

Taking these interpretations together – since Paul's words may be deliberately ambiguous – we find the reason why we are to have compassion on those who may be our enemies. Christ will be their judge; we are not. In Romans 12:17–20, Paul makes this the motive for heaping coals of fire on the heads of our enemies. Do not let your temper flare and take justice into your own hands.

RELATIONSHIP TO OURSELVES

Do not be anxious Paul urges us (v. 6). Within the space of three verses he appears to present us with two impossible tasks: constant rejoicing (v. 4) and now the rejection of anxiety (v. 6)! But the two are related; the joyful person is not likely to be dominated by anxiety; the anxiety-ridden spirit cannot be a joyful one. But how can we be delivered from anxiety?

The prescription is prayer. Anxiety cannot continue to breathe easily in an atmosphere suffused with prayer. This is not a trite statement, as Paul's expansion of it makes clear. He uses various terms for prayer (*prayer, petition, thanksgiving, requests*). He is speaking about the careful, patient spreading of our needs before God, detailing our situation and our anxieties. This is what it means to cast our burdens on the Lord in the assurance that he will sustain us (*Psa.* 55:2).

Notice too that Paul includes thanksgiving in his many-sided description, for the prayer of which he is thinking is not merely a listing of needs, but an opening of the heart to God which includes praising him for all that he is and has done for us.

It is clear, now, why paralysing anxiety cannot co-exist with prayer; the heart that has unburdened itself, and has been retuned to a spirit of praise cannot remain permanently anxious.

The praying Christian discovers that the mysterious *peace of God, which transcends all understanding* serves to *guard* our *hearts* and *minds in Christ* (v. 7). Paul speaks about this peace as though it were a military garrison – an apt picture for Christians in Philippi which itself was constantly guarded by a garrison of Roman soldiers.

The apostle is saying: God himself is the *God of peace* (v. 9); it is the atmosphere of heaven. You are in a world full of trouble and anxiety, far from the heavenly city of which you are a citizen. But

God sends a garrison of peace to guard you while you are away from your homeland.

Yes, both joy and peace are possible, even in a world like this. But they can be preserved only by a mind that is well-stocked with grace.

In our modern world many people seek freedom from anxiety by trying to empty their minds; Paul teaches us that true peace can be ours only when our minds are properly filled. He points the Philippians to the store from which they can furnish their minds: things that are *true, noble, right, pure, lovely, admirable, excellent or praiseworthy*. A mind full of these will leave little room for anxiety-producing, peace-disrupting and joy-destroying thoughts.

How can our minds thus be trained? Again Paul answers: by allowing our lives to be shaped by apostolic example and apostolic teaching (v. 9). The kind of Bible study in which we are presently engaged is itself the prescription the apostle provides. Take it, regularly, and we will enjoy the peace of God which comes to us from the God of peace (v. 9).

25

Learning Contentment

I rejoice greatly in the Lord that at last you have renewed your concern for me. Indeed, you have been concerned, but you had no opportunity to show it. I am not saying this because I am in need, for I have learned to be content whatever the circumstances. I know what it is to be in need, and I know what it is to have plenty. I have learned the secret of being content in any and every situation, whether well fed or hungry, whether living in plenty or in want. I can do everything through him who gives me strength (Phil. 4:10–13).

The centrepiece of Paul's letter to the Philippians is found in the exposition of the mind of Christ which he applies in different ways. Here, as elsewhere, he wants to train his readers to think Christianly in order that they may live faithfully. Even in the closing section of the letter, when the contents naturally take on a more varied character, we discover Paul returning to this idea. How we think about Christ, about others, and about our personal circumstances is bound to be a determining factor in how we live the Christian life.

The apostle has been urging the Philippians to rejoice. Now he tells them that he himself has a particular reason to rejoice: *at last you have renewed your concern* [he uses the verb 'to think' once more] *for me* (v. 10).

CONCERNED AT LAST?

The tone of these words has sometimes been misunderstood by readers of this letter. Isolated from other considerations they might be read as a none-too-veiled rebuke – like a young person receiving a letter from an aunt saying 'it was nice to hear from you – at last – and to know you received the present I sent you last year'!

But it is inconceivable that Paul is here rebuking his dear friends. He prays for them with joy (1:4); he is thankful for their partnership in the gospel (1:5); he longs for them and loves them all (1:8; 4:1); they are his brothers in Christ, his joy and crown (4:1); he rejoices in their gift (4:10).

Another explanation for Paul's *at last* is necessary. It may simply be a statement of fact – they had not been able to express their *concern* for some time, as in fact he goes on to say (v. 10). It is even possible that we should put the phrase in quotation marks. It is easy to imagine that the message which Epaphroditus brought from the Philippians – along with their financial gift – whether by letter or word of mouth, included the statement 'At last we are able to send these gifts to you . . .'

Paul elsewhere speaks about having 'robbed' the Macedonians (*2 Cor.* 11:8; presumably the Philippians in particular) in order to continue his ministry to the Corinthians. We know, too, that he was concerned that he should not profit personally from the finances supporting the apostolic mission, lest an accusation of self-seeking damage his integrity. He even seems to have discouraged individuals and churches from helping him financially for this reason (see *1 Cor.* 9:12). He insisted that the free grace of God be freely preached (*1 Cor.* 9:18). In addition he was probably very concerned lest he should give the Philippians the impression that he expected further gifts from them. He was not *in need* (v. 11).

It is never easy for Christ's servants to accept personal gifts, even when they are in need of them. They are naturally sensitive to rumours spreading that they are 'in it [i.e., the service of the gospel] for the money'. It would be perverse of us, however, if we made that a reason for closing our hearts to those who have made considerable financial as well as personal sacrifices in order to serve Christ. We need to learn the generous spirit of the Philippians, even if we cause embarrassment to those to whom we are generous! We must respect their sensitivity; but we must also be given the opportunity to discover that it is more blessed to give than to receive (*Acts* 20:35).

Paul was not *in need* (v. 11). That was true in the financial sense. But even if he had been in need, he would not have been discontented. He had learned how to cope with life *whatever the circumstances.*

Poverty and plenty had both been Paul's companion during his Christian life. There were times when his needs had been generously supplied; at other times he had 'known hunger and thirst and . . . often gone without food . . . been cold and naked' (*2 Cor.* 11:27). But he knew *the secret of being content* (v. 12) in such diverse conditions.

PAUL'S SECRET

What was – and is – this secret? *I can do everything through him* [i.e., in him] *who gives me strength* (v. 13). Do not isolate these words from their context. Paul is not saying that he could do anything to which he set his mind. The 'everything' refers in the first place to coping with need or plenty. The apostle's words are better translated 'in him'. It is 'in Christ' that he has learned to do this.

These are rich words of encouragement; they teach us that it is possible, by the grace of God, *to be content,* even in a world like this where we face trial, difficulty and deprivation. They are also words of experience, indicating that the contentment Paul describes is not to be confused with our natural temperament (Christians, like others, have higher and lower tolerance levels, and we may all too easily confuse the former with true contentment). No; spiritual contentment needs to be *learned,* and usually is so through hard or testing experiences.

Chiefly these are words of wise instruction, because they teach us that the contentment we may experience in this world does not depend upon anything that it alone has to offer us. It is only 'in Christ' that we can learn to be content.

In the phrase 'in Christ' the preposition 'in' seems to include the other prepositions the New Testament uses to describe the Christian's relationship to his Lord. Our contentment comes *from* Christ. It is through his work in our hearts by his Spirit that such contentment is given birth and grows. Christ himself was the supremely contented man: he fed on doing his Father's will and was contented with it (*John* 4:34). The Spirit of Jesus dwells in us to produce similar contentment.

Our contentment is also *for* Christ, in the sense that, with Paul, for Christ's sake we are prepared to lose all things so long as we are 'found in him' (*Phil.* 3:9).

More than that, it is a contentment *with* Christ. Only because he is with us can we be content. Paul had learned to be content in Christ particularly in the sense that possessing Christ had brought him a contentment which was independent of his immediate situation. Paul was content to have Christ – period. That is possible only for the Christian who knows the meaning of 'the surpassing greatness of knowing Christ Jesus my Lord' and in that light counts other things to be 'rubbish' by comparison (3:8).

For Paul contentment is not found in creating our own security, but by abandoning our security to Jesus Christ! He brings that out by the word he uses which our versions translate 'content' (v. 11). It is the term used in Greek philosophy for the virtue of self-sufficiency or independence. That was regarded as the highest of personal attainments, since it seemed to involve freedom from needs and weaknesses which might make us dependent on others. Paul, however, is not speaking about his sense of self-sufficiency. He was completely dependent on another, Jesus Christ. The difference between secular virtue and wisdom and biblical virtue and wisdom could hardly be more clearly described.

When he was weak, Christ made Paul strong; when he was empty, Christ filled him with his power; when he was poor, Christ made him rich. In *whatever . . . circumstances*, in Christ he had learned to be content. Since Christ meant more to him than life itself, how could it be otherwise?

Christians today live in a society which is permeated by a spirit of discontentment. Greed has destroyed gratitude, getting has replaced giving. But in the pursuit of self-sufficiency we have lost our way. We have developed spirits driven forwards to gain more, incapable of slowing, stopping and remembering that those who sow the wind reap the whirlwind. That ethos can easily influence Christians too. It is time to pause and to ask: 'Am I content, in Christ?' If not, it is the first thing I need to begin to relearn.

26

Partnership in the Gospel

Yet it was good of you to share in my troubles. Moreover, as you Philippians know, in the early days of your acquaintance with the gospel, when I set out from Macedonia, not one church shared with me in the matter of giving and receiving, except you only; for even when I was in Thessalonica, you sent me aid again and again when I was in need. Not that I am looking for a gift, but I am looking for what may be credited to your account. I have received full payment and even more. I am amply supplied, now that I have received from Epaphroditus the gifts you sent. They are a fragrant offering, an acceptable sacrifice, pleasing to God. And my God will meet all your needs according to his glorious riches in Christ Jesus. To our God and Father be glory for ever and ever. Amen (Phil. 4:14–20).

Paul gave the work of the gospel priority over his own personal comfort. But, as the previous verses have made clear, he did not do so with a mean spirit. In fact he had become an increasingly contented and generous man. Discontented with himself he remained – he was not yet perfect! (3:12) – but he was increasingly contented with Christ. Christ had come to mean more and more to him, worth losing all for (3:7–8), worth living for and dying for (1:21).

Paul emphasises this rigorous commitment, but his spirituality is not of the inhuman variety. While he lacks nothing, being content in Christ, he also wants his Philippian friends to know that he deeply appreciates their gift, and that it has been a means of blessing to him. His explanation of why this is so is particularly interesting and dominates the closing verses of his letter.

What do you say in a thank-you letter when you have received a gift? Ordinarily we might thank the giver, praise the gift and (if we can safely do so!) say what we have done with it. Paul does that, in part. He is aware of the fact that the love of the Philippians for him had been long-standing as well as outstanding. From the *early days* of the church's existence they supported the apostolic mission; they were, in fact, the only church that did so when he *set out from Macedonia* (v. 14). When he was evangelising in Thessalonica they had helped him *again and again* (v. 16). His gratitude for this was certainly genuine. Other congregations caused him on-going head-aches; the Philippians, whatever their present problems, had been more of a support than a burden to him; they had helped him in his work rather than given him more work in trying to help them.

But Paul has a deeper gratitude. In a sense he says very little about the content or usefulness of the gift he has received; he is more concerned with the spiritual commitment it expresses, the spiritual bond it creates, and the spiritual blessing to which it will lead.

GIVING AND RECEIVING

The Philippians had been willing to enter into partnership with Paul in the *troubles* (v. 14) or afflictions which he had experienced. They were not merely supporters, far less financiers; they were yoked together with him, sharing as they were able in his sufferings and in the relief of them. Paul is hinting that these Christians were prepared to experience financial deprivation in order to bring comfort to him when he had been deprived of his freedom.

This special relationship was one of *giving and receiving* (v. 15). It was a partnership, each partner contributing something different to the other. Thus viewed, the Philippians would never become jealous of Paul's status or gifts, nor would Paul complain that he alone bore the burden of Christian ministry. It is an ideal description of the relationships we ought to foster among our-selves. Ministers and people, missionaries and their supporting congregations alike should learn from Paul's example that there is no such thing as a one-man-ministry or -missionary.

Not only did Paul have a deeper gratitude, he had a greater

vision: *I am looking for what may be credited to your account* (v. 17). As far as he was concerned the Philippians had done everything that could possibly be expected of them. He had *received full payment* (v. 18; the Greek word is found on ancient receipts in the same way ours are stamped 'paid in full'). He was more interested in the blessing they would gain by giving than the relief he might experience by the gift. Here is an extraordinary fruit of grace: a gift-getter who is thankful chiefly for what the gift tells him about the gift-givers!

SACRIFICIAL GIVING

But what is it that may be *credited* to the Philippians' *account?* Are they earning merit by these good deeds? Paul tells us: *They are a fragrant offering, an acceptable sacrifice, pleasing to God* (v. 18).

These words are reminiscent of the response of God to the sacrifice made by Noah after the flood (*Gen.* 9:20–21). The sacrifice was not the means of Noah's salvation, nor of earning favour with God; it was an expression of gratitude for the salvation God had given him and his family. It was a sacrifice of praise! It drew forth the loving compassion and faithfulness of God to his weak children. Similarly, Jesus' death was a sacrifice of atonement, but it was also an expression of his loving obedience to his Father and therefore a fragrant offering to him (*Eph.* 5:2).

This, then, for Paul is the wonderful thing about the Philippians' *gifts* (v. 18): they reflect the ministry of all believers as priests before the Lord. Not only have they exercised the priesthood of all believers in praying for Paul; their gifts have been like thank-offerings to the Lord, with which he has been pleased. What a delight it was to the apostle to think that these Christians he had nurtured were also doing things that were a delight to the Lord!

To give sacrificially, as the Philippians did, means that we may be in danger of impoverishing ourselves (cf. *2 Cor.* 11:8). Paul has some words of encouragement: their needs will be supplied, in turn, by the Lord, *according to his glorious riches* (v. 19). He is reminding them of the principle, illustrated frequently throughout Scripture, but powerfully enunciated by Jesus himself: whatever we yield up to him we will regain again and again (*Luke* 18:28–30).

All the riches of Christ's heavenly resources are available to us. He is never in debt to any of his children. The Philippians were seeking to put the kingdom of God and its advance first in their lives; that was why they gave so lovingly to Paul. Paul was assuring them, on the basis of Jesus' teaching and also out of his own experience, that everything they needed would be provided (*Matt.* 6:33).

In response to these thoughts, Paul breaks into praise. Prisoner he may be, but his soul cannot be contained by walls. It rises in adoration to his God and Father, who is also the God and Father of the Philippians. To him be *glory for ever and ever* (v. 20).

These verses, so casual at first sight, provide us with material for a catechism which will help us assess our concern for the Lord, his servants and the advance of his kingdom. It may be a challenging exercise to reflect on the answers we would give.

Question 1: Am I really concerned for the welfare of the Lord's servants? If they have material needs, do I simply shrug my shoulders and say, 'They didn't *need* to become involved in poorly supported (or poorly remunerated) Christian service'? But they did need to, didn't they? Otherwise they would have been disobeying their Lord, and yours.

Question 2: Do I regard my Christian stewardship, particularly although not exclusively of money, as a partnership? Or do I see it only as an investment with no return, a one-way-relationship (I give, they get)?

Question 3: Do I really believe that God will supply what I need if I give sacrificially? Or do I always give in such a way that sacrifice will be avoided? Do I see that generous giving is not the same thing as sacrificial giving (I can give generously, yet not sacrificially)?

Question 4: Do I really want to live and give, pray and share with others in such a way that glory will be seen to come to our God and Father by the way his people (i) love each other, (ii) support each other's ministries, and (iii) depend on the Lord's provision so that it becomes clear that the power and the glory are his and not ours?

When, with Paul and the Philippians, we see that our chief end is to glorify God then we will also discover what it means to enjoy him for ever.

27

Yours Sincerely, Paul

*Greet all the saints in Christ Jesus. The brothers who are with
me send greetings. All the saints send you greetings, especially
those who belong to Caesar's household. The grace of the
Lord Jesus Christ be with your spirit. Amen* (Phil. 4:21–23).

Paul's letters normally begin with a greeting in which he wishes
the blessings of grace and peace to his readers; they end with
further greetings and an apostolic benediction. Philippians is no
exception.

In fact there are three greetings: from Paul himself to all the
Christians; then from the Christians who are with him; thirdly
from the whole church in Rome (if indeed his imprisonment was
in the capital of the Empire).

By this stage in our study of a biblical book we are tempted to
note such things only with a final brief glance at the page, before
we move on to the more important business of a fresh area of study.
There is surely little or nothing to learn here. But *all* Scripture is
God-breathed and is, therefore, 'useful for teaching, rebuking,
correcting and training in righteousness' (*2 Tim.* 3:16). This is just
as true of the closing words of Paul's letters as it is of their opening
sentences!

GREETINGS FROM PAUL

The apostle wanted *greetings* to be conveyed to all the Christians
in Philippi. This command may be specifically addressed to the

'overseers and deacons' mentioned in 1:1. They are to make sure that everyone in the church hears the message: 'Paul has written to us; he wants us all to know that he is thinking of us and praying for our work. He specifically sends his greetings to all of us!'

A colourless enough ending, we might think, until we remember one of the great burdens of this letter: healing divisions in a fellowship. Paul wants *all the saints,* however they have aligned themselves over the Euodia–Syntyche disagreement, to know that he loves, cares for, and prays for each one of them, without distinction. Nor must they misunderstand some of the strong words he has written (for example about the 'dogs' in 3:2); these are expressions of his passionate concern to see his dear Philippian friends stand firm and make progress in the gospel.

This catholic spirit is a beautiful grace. But it is not as common among Christians as it ought to be. Yes, Paul knew that the Christians in Philippi did not all show the same maturity of understanding and judgment (see 3:15). But his love was not determined by their maturity so much as by the fact that they were his spiritual family. 'Blood is thicker than water' goes the saying; it is all the more so when the blood which binds us together is the precious blood of Christ (*1 Pet.* 1:18-19).

GREETINGS *VIA* PAUL

Paul also passed on *greetings* from *the brothers* who were with him (v. 21), that is those who were associated with him, perhaps even living with him, during his imprisonment. These may well include some of the Christians he mentions towards the end of the Letter to the Colossians (*Col.* 4:7–14). He gladly associates them with himself, perhaps to reassure his friends that he is not alone.

There is something touching about the thought of Paul's supporters asking him to send their greetings to their fellow-Christians, whether they knew them personally or not. They had heard Paul's fervent and joyful prayers for the Philippians and therefore had some sense of how much they meant to the apostle (1:3–4); they must have felt that they knew that distant congregation already.

These greetings, therefore, may have their origin in times of corporate prayer. That is the easiest, and the best place to get to know Christians we have never met. The love that is expressed here is an indication of how real and vital that knowledge can be. Paul's companions must have looked forward eagerly to the prospect of meeting his 'joy and crown' (4:1), either here or hereafter.

Final greetings are also passed on by Paul from *those who belong to Caesar's household* (v. 22). These were probably slaves or freedmen who worked in the Roman civil service. It is thrilling to think that already the gospel had penetrated the machinery of government and that some of the power-brokers in the ancient world were coming into contact with humble Christians shining like stars in the universe (2:15).

In the providence of God, some of these civil servants might have had knowledge of their counterparts in the Roman colony of Philippi. Perhaps they had even handled the same official documents. How encouraging also for some of the Philippian Christians (perhaps struggling with the implications of being a Christian citizen and a Christian civil servant) to remember that other believers were facing similar, or even more critical, situations in the capital city itself.

In prison Paul's testimony had penetrated the palace guard (1:13); in the corridors of the power of the Empire another kingdom was arising! Christ was building his church even where the gates of Hades would seek to destroy it (*Matt.* 16:18). This was, after all, the late 50s or early 60s A.D. It was to none other than Nero that Paul had appealed (*Acts* 25:10–11), leading to his present imprisonment. It would not be long before the persecution of the church would erupt. But the Empire whose outposts were in Rome and in Philippi would remain and grow.

Rome, on the other hand, would crumble. Already there were hints that this would be the case; cracks were appearing in the capital city: Christ's men and women were there.

THE BENEDICTION

The grace of the Lord Jesus Christ be with your spirit writes Paul (v. 23), returning to the theme of his opening greetings. Perhaps significantly, Paul couples a singular noun (*spirit*, singular) with a plural pronoun (*your*, plural): *your spirit* rather than 'your spirits'. The choice of words may have no significance. Paul may simply be praying for each member's spirit to know Christ's grace. It is, however, tempting to think that there is here a final echo of his earlier words:

> Whatever happens, conduct yourselves in a manner worthy of the gospel of Christ. Then, whether I come and see you or only hear about you in my absence, I will know that you *stand firm in one spirit*, contending as one man for the faith of the gospel (1:27).

Such unity was certainly Paul's prayer. Its only possible origin is in the grace of the Lord Jesus Christ. That was true in the first century, for the Philippians. It is no less true today, for us.

Group Study Guide

SCHEME FOR GROUP BIBLE STUDY
(Covering 13 Weeks)

	Study Passage	Chapters
1.	Philippians 1:1–4	1 and 2
2.	Philippians 1:5–11	3 and 4
3.	Philippians 1:12–18a	5 and 6
4.	Philippians 1:18b–26	7 and 8
5.	Philippians 1:27–2:4	9 and 10
6.	Philippians 2:5–11	11 and 12
7.	Philippians 2:12–18	13 and 14
8.	Philippians 2:19–30	15 and 16
9.	Philippians 3:1–11	17, 18 and 19
10.	Philippians 3:12–19	20 and 21
11.	Philippians 3:20–4:3	22 and 23
12.	Philippians 4:4–13	24 and 25
13.	Philippians 4:14–23	26 and 27

This Study Guide has been prepared for group Bible study, but it can also be used individually. Those who use it on their own may find it helpful to keep a notebook of their responses.

The way in which group Bible studies are led can greatly enhance their value. A well-conducted study will appear as though it has been easy to lead, but that is usually because the leader has worked hard and planned well. Clear aims are essential.

AIMS

In all Bible study, individual or corporate, we have several aims:

1. To gain an understanding of the original meaning of the particular passage of Scripture.

2. To apply this to ourselves and our own situation.

3. To develop some specific ways of putting the biblical teaching into practice.

2 Timothy 3:16–17 provides a helpful structure. Paul says that Scripture is useful for:

   (i)   teaching us;

  (ii)   rebuking us;

 (iii)   correcting, or changing us;

 (iv)   training us in righteousness.

Consequently, in studying any passage of Scripture, we should always have in mind these questions:

What does this passage teach us (about God, ourselves, etc.)?

Does it rebuke us in some way?

How can its teaching transform us?

What equipment does it give us for serving Christ?

In fact these four questions alone would provide a safe guide in any Bible study.

PRINCIPLES

In group Bible study we meet in order to learn about God's word and ways 'together with all the saints' (*Eph.* 3:18). But our own experience, as well as Scripture, tells us that the saints are not always what they are called to be in every situation – including group Bible study! Leaders ordinarily have to work hard and prepare well if the work of the group is to be spiritually profitable. The following guidelines for leaders may help to make this a reality.

Preparation:

1. Study and understand the passage yourself. The better prepared and more sure of the direction of the study you are, the more likely it is that the group will have a beneficial and enjoyable study.

Ask: What are the main things this passage is saying? How can this be made clear? This is not the same question as the more common 'What does this passage "say to you"?' which expects a personal reaction rather than an exposition of the passage. Be clear about that distinction yourself and work at making it clear in the group study.

2. On the basis of your own study form a clear idea *before* the group meets of (i) the main theme(s) of the passage which should be opened out for discussion, and (ii) some general conclusions the group ought to reach as a result of the study. Here the questions which arise from 2 Timothy 3:16–17 should act as our guide.

3. The guidelines and questions which follow may help to provide a general framework for each discussion; leaders should use them as starting places which can be further developed. It is usually helpful to have a specific goal or theme in mind for group discussion, and one is suggested for each study. But even more important than tracing a single theme is understanding the teaching and the implications of the passage.

Leading the Group:

1. Announce the passage and theme for the study and begin with prayer. In group studies it may be helpful to invite a different person to lead in prayer each time you meet.

2. Introduce the passage and theme, briefly reminding people of its outline, and highlighting the content of each subsidiary section.

3. Lead the group through the discussion questions. Use your own if you are comfortable in doing so; those provided may be used, developing them with your own points. As discussion proceeds, continue to encourage the group first of all to discuss the significance of the passage (teaching) and only then its application

(meaning for us). It may be helpful to write important points and applications on a board by way of summary as well as visual aid.

4.   At the end of each meeting remind members of the group of its assignments for the next meeting and encourage them to come prepared. Be sufficiently prepared as the leader to give specific assignments to individuals or even couples or groups to come with specific contributions ('John, would you try to find out something about the Praetorian Guard for the next meeting?' 'Betty, would you see what you can find out about the different ways in which Philippians 2:5–11 has been interpreted?').

5.   Remember that you are the leader of the group! Encourage clear contributions and do not be embarrassed to ask someone to explain what they have said more fully, or to help them to do so ('Do you mean . . . ?').

Most groups include the 'over-talkative', the 'over-silent' and the 'red-herring raisers'! Leaders must control the first, encourage the second and redirect the third! Each leader will develop his or her own most natural way of doing that; but it will be helpful to think out what that is before the occasion arises! The first two groups can be helped by some judicious direction of questions to specific individuals or even groups (e.g., 'How do those who are not working outside of the home apply this?' 'Jane, you know something about this from personal experience . . .'); the third by redirecting the discussion to the passage itself ('That is an interesting point, but isn't it true that this passage really concentrates on . . . ?'). It may be helpful to break the group up into smaller groups sometimes, giving each sub-group specific points to discuss and to report back on. A wise arranging of these smaller groups may also help each member to participate.

More important than any techniques we may develop is the help of the Spirit to help us to understand and to apply the Scriptures. Have and encourage a humble, prayerful spirit.

6.   Keep faith with the schedule; it is better that some of the group wished the study could have been longer than that others are inconvenienced by it stretching beyond the time limits set.

7.   Close in prayer. As time permits, spend the closing minutes in corporate prayer, encouraging the group to apply what they have learned in praise and thanks, intercession and petition.

STUDY 1: Philippians 1:1–5

AIM: To see the relationship between Paul and the church at Philippi as an example and challenge to our relationship to the church and to each other.

1. 'Many Christians find Philippians the most attractive of all Paul's letters' (p. 1). Has that been the experience of those who have read the letter before? What particular things in it stick out in the memory as being important? Note them down and return to the list in the last study.

2. Four things are said to characterise the first readers of this letter. What are they? In one sense these things embrace all of our relationships (in ourselves, to Christ, in our context, to Christian leaders). In what ways does Paul's teaching about these relationships challenge us?

3. These Christians were 'in Christ', but 'at Philippi'. From what you know of Philippi (see *Acts* 16:11–40 and the introduction on pp. xi–xvi) what difficulties and opportunities did that present to them?

4. Paul had a special responsibility for the Philippian church as a founding apostle. But the kind of love for the church which he expresses in verses 3–5 derives from a Christian heart, not from an office in the church. What can we learn from his example (*1 Cor.* 4:16; 11:1)?

5. Discuss the comment: 'It is . . . never money wasted when we send people to encourage missionaries as well as provide them with financial support' (p. 8).

6. The Philippians were partners with Paul in his work. What three things do we need to notice about this partnership? Can you add to this? What practical things can you do (as an individual or fellowship) to follow their example?

7. Is it significant that Paul begins with gratitude rather than complaints? Why do some of us instinctively do the reverse whenever we mention other Christians? Does the way in which Paul thinks of the Philippians help here?

FOR STUDY 2: Read Philippians 1:5–11 and chapters 3 and 4.

STUDY 2: Philippians 1:5–11

AIM: To explore the bonds of grace and love that are possible among Christians.

1. Paul speaks about God beginning the work in the Philippians (v. 6). Look again at Acts 16:6–40 and list the different evidences of this.

2. On what basis is Paul confident that God will complete this work? What other passages in his writings shed light on this confidence?

3. In verses 7 and 8 Paul says the Philippians are (i) in his heart; (ii) share his grace, and (iii) longed for with the affection of Christ. How would the presence of these qualities make a difference in our fellowship?

4. Is it fair to charge some Christians with 'fickleness'? Are there serious evidences of it? Is it more predominant now than in previous generations of Christians? If so, why?

5. 'The bonds of grace are strengthened by adversity' (p. 12). How was this true for Paul? How have you experienced that?

6. Paul's prayer (vv. 9–11) focuses on several things. What are they? Explain what you think he means by (i) knowledge; (ii) insight. What is the difference between this and knowledge? (iii) the fruit of righteousness.
    How do you think Paul would have expected this prayer to be answered – how do we grow in these graces?

7. Examine the content of Paul's prayer (cf. also *Eph.* 1:15–21 and *Col.* 1:9–12) and compare it with the content of your own prayers for others. Are there differences? What are they? Why do they exist? What can we learn from these prayers to help us to pray?

FOR STUDY 3: Read Philippians 1:12–18a and chapters 4 and 5.

AIM: To be aware of the effects our attitudes have on our Christian service.

1. 'Paul . . . knew that God invariably means to bring new blessings out of the trials and difficulties his servants experience' (p. 18). How did Paul know this? In what other passages does he emphasise it? Is the same principle illustrated in the lives of others in Scripture? What difference does this make to our attitude to adversity?

2. How should we respond when – unlike Paul's experience here – it does not become clear why we experience adversity?
    How can it become evident in our everyday life that, like Paul, we experience everything 'for Christ' (v. 13)?

3. Paul saw that his response to his circumstances influenced others. Did Paul allow that possibility to influence his behaviour here or at other times?

4. In what contexts is it a biblical principle that the reaction of others should influence our behaviour (see *Rom.* 14:1–15:3; *1 Cor.* 8:1–13)? What principles for Christian conduct are involved here?

5. Paul warns us here against 'selfish ambition' (v. 17). In what ways is that a danger today in Christian service? How would it manifest itself?

6. How can we learn to have Paul's balance (rejoicing that Christ is preached despite false motives, vv. 15–18)?

7. What are some of the causes of false motives in our own Christian service, and how can we deal with them?

8. 'We must reserve in our hearts a sanctuary of love for Jesus Christ – a sanctuary from which everything but trust in him and love for him is barred' (p. 24). Discuss this idea.

FOR STUDY 4: Read Philippians 1:18b–26 and chapters 7 and 8.

STUDY 4: Philippians 1:18b–26

AIM: To recognise the mutual dependence of Christians in the present age, and the glorious prospect which awaits them in the future.

1. Paul anticipates his deliverance (v. 19) as a result of (i) prayer and (ii) the help of the Spirit. Why both? What other indications are there in Paul's letters that he relies on his fellow-Christians?

2. How do you think the Philippians prayed for Paul to be helped?
   Why do you think Paul is concerned here lest he should be ashamed (v. 20)?

3. 'He reserves the best of his gifts for the time of our greatest need' (p. 27). How was that true for Paul? Has it been true in any special way for you?

4. What was 'more important than life' to Paul (p. 27) and how can it be a mark of our lives also?

5. Paul indicates that he struggled to reach the conclusion he describes in verses 23–26. How do we learn to tell the difference between our natural inclinations and the will of God?

6. What teaching does the New Testament give on what happens to the believer at death?

7. Discuss the application of these verses to 'Christians who have few gifts, or are weakened by illness, or who have grown frail in old age' (p. 32). How can we strengthen our anticipation of being with Christ?

FOR STUDY 5: Read Philippians 1:27–2:4 and chapters 9 and 10.

STUDY 5: Philippians 1:27–2:4

AIM: To become more aware of both the responsibilities and the privileges which are ours in Christ.

1.   Paul urged the Philippians to a lifestyle 'worthy of the gospel of Christ' (1:27). Later (2:1–18) he makes specific application of what this means. But here it implies to 'live as a citizen' (p. 34). What parallels are implied between citizenship and Christian living?

2.   In what ways do you find opposition to your Christian life and witness intimidating? Does Paul give some hints in this passage about how the fear of intimidation may be overcome?

3.   In Philippians 1:28, Paul speaks about an aspect of Christian witness that we rarely think about. Compare 2 Corinthians 2:15–16. What do these passages lead us to expect as the result of our witness?

4.   Does it make any difference to the Christian who suffers to see suffering as a gift (v. 29)?

5.   List Paul's four 'ifs' (Phil. 2:1–2; pp. 38–39). In what ways are you conscious of these privileges in your life? What is the connection between them and what follows in verses 2–4?

6.   Since we are proud by nature, how can we learn to 'do nothing out of . . . vain conceit' and 'in humility count others better' (v. 3)?

7.   The New Testament places a great deal of emphasis on the unity of Christians (e.g., v. 2). Why? What implications does this carry for our fellowship?

FOR STUDY 6: Read Philippians 2:5–11 and chapters 11 and 12.

STUDY 6: Philippians 2:5–11

AIM: To come to a better understanding of the person and work of Jesus Christ.

1. What is the function of these verses in the context of Philippians 2?

2. From one point of view these verses might seem to be the easiest to study in Paul's letter. But in some ways they are the most difficult, despite being so important and so deeply loved. Can you think why this is?

3. In verses 6–8, trace the steps in Christ's self-humbling. What does it mean for you to share this 'mind of Christ'?

4. Christ did not 'jealously guard his rights' (p. 43). In a sense, however, Paul had 'stood on his rights' as a Roman citizen in Philippi (see Acts 16:37 and introduction). Was he behaving in a self-centred fashion at that point? What should the attitude of a Christian be to his or her 'rights', and to 'civil rights'?

5. It is claimed that verses 9–11 set out Christ's divine identity. How would you answer someone who responded: 'But these verses teach that Jesus became divine, not that he was always God!'?

6. 'The love of his Father for him made his exaltation the inevitable consequence of his humiliation' (p. 49).
   Are there other New Testament passages which teach us about the Father's love for his Son? What do they add to the teaching of these verses?

7. In what ways should Paul's teaching on Christ's incarnation transform our lives?

FOR STUDY 7: Read Philippians 2:12–18 and chapters 13 and 14.

STUDY 7: Philippians 2:12–18

AIM: To understand what it means to 'work out' our salvation.

1. Note the stress on the importance of the word 'therefore' for Paul (v. 2). What is its significance? Are there other passages which underline this principle?

2. Why are we faithful when certain people are with us, but less so in their absence?

3. What is the difference between working 'for' and working 'out' our salvation? In what ways can we say that 'God . . . works in you to will and to act according to his good purpose' (v. 13)?
    Is there really a place for 'fear and trembling' in your Christian life?

4. Using Paul's comparison between God's people after the exodus and the temptations Christians face, what would you suggest are the main reasons why Christians too often complain and argue? How can we prevent that?

5. Consider Paul's unique description of Christians in verse 15 as a goal for your own life. What changes need to take place in order for Paul's description to be true of us? In what ways do we hold out the word of life? In what ways do we fail to do so?

6. Trace the theme of sacrifice through Philippians 2:5–11 and 2:17. How important an element is it in the Christian life?

FOR STUDY 8: Read Philippians 2:19–30 and chapters 15 and 16.

STUDY 8: Philippians 2:19–30

AIM: To study examples of true Christian character and to imitate them.

1.   Paul described his relationship with Timothy as 'a son with his father'. In the light of this passage and 2 Tim. 1:1–7 and 3:10–17, what seem to have been the chief features of this 'discipling relationship'?

2.   In what ways do Paul's words in 2:21 have relevance to us today?

3.   The model disciple is 'delivered from the bondage of self-obsession . . . free to live in self-forgetfulness . . . delighting to be the servants of others' (p. 64). How are such qualities developed?

4.   What applications can be made from thinking about Epaphroditus as a missionary returned home?

5.   Is it true that there is 'all too little generosity of heart in our praise of other Christians' (p. 66)? How can we develop gratitude and admiration for the gifts and graces of others?

6.   Have you ever come across the view of Christian life and service, 'if it takes effort it cannot be the fruit of the Spirit's presence' (p. 67)? How do you respond to it?

7.   Epaphroditus had risked his life, and had nearly died. How do we strike the balance between wisdom and risk-taking for Christ? Are there principles in Scripture to guide us? Do we have a tendency to avoid pain under the pretence of 'the balanced Christian life'?

8.   Think of two other Christians, from history, or whom you have known and admired. What aspects of their Christian lives most impressed you and why? In what ways can you emulate them?

FOR STUDY 9: Read Philippians 3:1–11 and chapters 17, 18, and 19.

STUDY 9: Philippians 3:1–11

AIM: To understand what is involved in having a truly Christian ambition for our lives.

1. How can we obey the command to 'rejoice in the Lord' (v. 1)?

2. In this section, Paul writes some of his strongest words against false teachers. How can his fierce language be justified? Should we use it?

3. What are the practical implications of the three characteristics of true Christians which Paul lists in verse 3?

4. In what ways are we tempted to rely for our standing before God on things in our background?

5. The martyr Stephen may have had a considerable impact on Paul, even if Paul did not notice it at the time (p. 77). Do other passages of Scripture support or illustrate this? What lessons can we learn from this?

6. In what ways is the gospel 'a tremendous shock to the system' (p. 80)? In what ways does it continue to be this to the Christian who grows in an understanding of it?

7. Paul gained justification. But what is justification? How does Paul explain its significance in verse 9?

8. Express Paul's ambition (vv. 10–11) in your own words.

9. 'As we live in Christ our risen Saviour . . . he leads us on to *the fellowship of sharing in his sufferings*' (p. 82). What is the biblical basis for such a statement and what does it involve?

FOR STUDY 10: Read Philippians 3:12–19 and chapters 20 and 21.

STUDY 10: Philippians 3:12–19

AIM: To consider the nature and role of goals in the Christian life.

1. Paul had clearly defined goals of at least three kinds: short-term, long-term and life-time. Think of your own life within these three perspectives. What goals should you be setting? Discuss what principles should be involved in setting them.

2. What are the distinctive principles which guide Christian goal-setting?

3. What was involved in Christ 'taking hold' of Paul (v. 13)?

4. Why, when Paul denied possessing it, have some Christians claimed 'perfection'? Paul seems to have believed that one of the marks of maturity is modesty about our spiritual progress. What is the explanation for this paradox?

5. If 'models' are valuable for living the Christian life, how can we be guided to follow the right ones?

6. How would we recognise someone who lives 'as an enemy of the cross of Christ'?

7. Why is self-indulgence a mark of counterfeit spirituality?

8. 'There is a cast of mind that betrays the message of the gospel' (p. 92). How can we (i) recognise this and (ii) avoid it?

FOR STUDY 11: Read Philippians 3:20–4:3 and chapters 22 and 23.

STUDY 11: Philippians 3:20–4:3

AIM: To understand that Christians live with a different perspective from the world on (i) the future and (ii) disagreements.

1. In what ways does the Christian inevitably 'stand out' as a citizen of heaven?

2. How would a frequent asking of the question, 'What future is there in the object of your devotion?' (p. 94) help us live the Christian life more faithfully?

3. 'Salvation is a process of transforming us into the likeness of Christ' (p. 95). Trace the stages in this process. Is this the way we normally think about themselves?
   In what ways do we fail to 'Live for the things that will last!' (p. 96)? Why?

4. What do you think are the most common reasons for divisions within the church?

5. 'How can two people who think differently be brought to think in the same way' (p. 99)?

6. How can we recognise and deal with pride as a cause of disagreement among Christians?

7. What are some of the potential dangers for a Christian fellowship when two of its prominent members seriously disagree? How can we minimise these dangers?

FOR STUDY 12: Read Philippians 4:4–13 and chapters 24 and 25.

STUDY 12: Philippians 4:4–13

AIM: To see how the gospel delivers us from anxiety and teaches us contentment.

1.   In the life of the Christian, what should be the relationship between mind, will and emotion? In what ways does this relationship tend to be disrupted? What are the consequences? How can we learn to order our lives properly?

2.   How can we promote joy in our lives?

3.   Gentleness, patience, and kindliness are all qualities Paul regards as essential in Christian living. How is Christ our example in these areas? Why are these graces minimised so frequently? How can we develop them?

4.   In what two senses may Christ be said to be 'near'? What are the implications the New Testament draws from this?

5.   Why is our society so anxiety-ridden? What are the characteristics of the prayer Paul describes as a remedy?

6.   'We need to learn the generous spirit of the Philippians, even if we cause embarrassment to those to whom we are generous' (p. 107). Respond to this comment.

7.   What are some of the things that make us discontented? How does Paul's teaching help us to be delivered from that spirit?

FOR STUDY 13: Read Philippians 4:14–23 and chapters 26 and 27.

STUDY 13: Philippians 4:14–23

AIM: To see how true spirituality affects our relationships with others.

1. Paul's 'spirituality is not of the inhuman variety' (p. 110). What does this mean? Is there a danger here to avoid? What indications do we have in Philippians (and also in Paul's other letters) that the work of the Spirit in sanctifying Paul made him more truly and fully human?

2. What applications does Paul's relationship to the Philippians (in 'giving and receiving') have today?

3. How can we practise the principle that 'there is no such thing as a one-man-ministry' (p. 111) without minimising the importance of the ministry of the word of God?

4. How are love and sacrifice related? Is it right ever to 'be in danger of impoverishing ourselves' (p. 112)?

5. Study and discuss the four questions in the 'catechism' (p. 113).

6. Contrast Paul's 'catholic' spirit – his love for all the Lord's people expressed in his final greetings – with the spirit of Diotrophes in 3 John verses 9–10. What do you see to imitate and to avoid?

7. Review the answers that were given to question 1 in the first study about lessons learned from previous studies in Philippians. What new lessons have been impressed on you in this study?

FOR FURTHER READING

The following books are recommended for study of Paul's Letter to the Philippians:

William Hendriksen: *A Commentary on the Epistle to the Philippians, Colossians and Philemon,* Banner of Truth Trust, Edinburgh, 1981 (the section on Philippians was originally published as a separate volume in 1962).

J. A. Motyer: *The Message of Philippians: Jesus our Joy* (The Bible Speaks Today series) InterVarsity Press, Leicester 1984 (earlier published under the title *The Richness of Christ* in 1966).

Moisés Silva: *Philippians* (Wycliffe Exegetical Commentary series), Moody Press, Chicago, Ill., 1988 (now published by Baker Book House, Grand Rapids, MI.).